Making the
Most of Your
401(k)

Also by Gordon K. Williamson:

LOW RISK INVESTING

100 BEST MUTUAL FUNDS YOU CAN BUY

Making the Most of Your

401(k)

Gordon K. Williamson

ADAMS MEDIA CORPORATION
Holbrook, Massachusetts

Published by Adams Media Corporation,
260 Center Street, Holbrook, MA 02343

ISBN: 1-55850-584-9

Printed in Canada.

J I H G F E D C B A

Library of Congress Cataloging-in-Publication Data
Making the most of your 401(k) / Gordon K. Williamson.
p.   cm.
Includes index.
ISBN 1-55850-584-9 (pbk.)
1. 401(k) plans. 2. Retirement income—United States—Planning.
I. Title.
HD7105.45.U6W55   1996
332.024'01—dc20   96-995
CIP

This publication is designed to provide accurate and authoritative information with regard to the subject matter covered. It is sold with the understanding that the publisher is not engaged in rendering legal, accounting, or other professional advice. If legal advice or other expert assistance is required, the services of a competent professional person should be sought.

> — From a *Declaration of Principles* jointly adopted by a
> Committee of the American Bar Association and a
> Committee of Publishers and Associations

*This book is available at quantity discounts for bulk purchases.
For information, call 1-800-872-5627.*

Visit our home page at http://www.adamsmedia.com

This book is dedicated
to all my clients.

Table of Contents

Introduction

According to a 1995 *New York Times*/CBS News poll, three out of four working Americans expect people their age to face a financial crisis when they retire. Over half of those polled say that they have not even begun to save for retirement. And many see themselves reaching old age without the company-paid pensions and Social Security that allowed their parents to live so comfortably.

People over fifty are still largely protected by the old system. But for everyone else, the security of Social Security is slipping away. This growing realization of just how unprepared they are is beginning to show up in public opinion polls. Twenty percent of working Americans have postponed their planned retirement dates. Forty percent of those with savings say that they started saving too late to adequately support themselves in old age.

Even though company pensions and Social Security are on the decline, over half of the working population still believes that these will be their major sources of income later in life. The change is especially hard on middle-income people earning $30,000 to $100,000. More than most any other income group, these people are relying heavily on promises made by their employers and Social Security.

Three-quarters of those workers who do have investments rarely buy or sell securities or shift savings from one mutual fund to another. These accounts, as a result of neglect and being too conservative, earn less than company pension funds managed by professionals.

There are a number of different kinds of retirement plans. You may be entitled to participate in one or more. One type of retirement account is known as a 401(k) plan. Whether or not you are entitled to invest in a 401(k) plan depends upon the policies of the company you work for.

During the past few years, the 401(k) plan has become the most popular company-sponsored way to save for retirement. Close to a third of those people who work and have a savings plan also have a 401(k). Unfortunately, the median 401(k) account has only $5,000 in it, according to the Pension Rights Center. According to pension experts, this figure represents a small fraction of the $500,000 to $1,000,000 people should have in a retirement plan in order to generate a $40,000 to $80,000 annual income.

One purpose of this book is to explain how 401(k) plans work, along with their advantages and their disadvantages. In addition to learning about this type of retirement plan, you will also learn how contributions are made, how distributions are determined, and how to make the best use of the 401(k) plan that you participate in.

The bulk of this book deals with the *investment* aspects of 401(k) plans. Although you may not have much latitude or voice in deciding the *kind* of retirement plan your company has or is thinking about adopting, chances are that you can decide how your contributions are invested. Your investment choices may range from the ultraconservative, such as money market accounts, to the very aggressive, such as a mutual fund that invests only in bullion and gold-mining stocks.

As you will learn, how much money you end up with and the amount of monthly income you will be receiving when you retire will largely depend upon *how* the money is invested originally, or periodically repositioned. Long term, whether you are in the XYZ Growth Fund or the ABC Growth Fund is not nearly as important as whether you should be in *any* growth mutual fund or stocks and, if so, to what degree.

You will learn about the different types of investments available to most 401(k) plan participants, how each one works, which ones should be part of your retirement plan, and which are best for nonretirement accounts.

When it comes to investing, most brokers and financial planners will tell you all the good attributes of a given invest-ment; this book will do the same, but also tell you all the risks involved. There are literally thousands of different investments out there. In fact, there are now more than 7,000 different mutual funds—and mutual funds are just one of several ways to invest.

I have been an investment adviser for over fifteen years. I am also one of the most highly trained brokers and counselors in the nation and have written twenty books on investing, retirement accounts, and estate planning. During the course of my career I have certainly made my fair share of mistakes (perhaps even more than my fair share). What I have learned over these years can benefit you immensely. As I have learned (sometimes the hard way), if you avoid the "bad stuff," you are about 75 percent of the way to doing a good job and hav-ing the right portfolio.

The main purpose of the book will be to teach you how to incorporate the information you will learn into your *overall* financial plan. You will learn how to look at your 401(k) opportunity as part of the *entire* picture, instead of looking at it in isolation—without considering your other holdings. It is this *portfolio* approach, looking at all parts of your investment savings, that should be the greatest benefit you will receive from this book.

As an active investment adviser, I deal in literally thousands of different investments. Since there are few, if any, investments that I do not have access to, I do not have to favor one kind or type of investment over another (e.g., if you sell Ford automobiles for a living, how objective can you be about GM or Toyota?). You would be amazed at the number of well-known publications, some of them household names, and financial talk-show hosts and authors who give biased advice that is not always in your best interest.

The material in this book is written from a neutral perspective. None of the research is based on a grant or fee received from a product group, brokerage firm, or any other source that might be less than neutral in its objectivity.

Since there is no "hidden agenda" here, you can be confident that the information and advice you receive in this book includes not only everything you need to make an informed decision, but also the necessary tools to make sure that you are not taken advantage of or misguided by someone because of that person's ignorance or the way he or she is compensated. When the subject of investments comes up, most people's eyes glaze over. Yet the world of investing can actually be fun and profitable. I hope that you will find this book not only informative, but interesting.

CHAPTER 1
How to Use This Book

The text of this book is divided into thirteen chapters, ranging in size from just a couple to several dozens of pages. It is intended for three types of readers: (1) those who have little, if any, knowledge about retirement planning and investments, (2) those who have read a book or two about investing or have attended investment seminars and are interested in how to integrate a 401(k) plan into their overall investment strategy, and (3) those who have little, if any, time to learn about 401(k) investing, and who want to know just what they need to know to make intelligent decisions.

You *should* read the entire book. However, if you do not have the time or interest, this first chapter can help you save time—by showing you which chapters or sections that either may be too basic for you or do not apply to your particular set of circumstances. A series of examples of typical investors is listed below. Look for the description that best fits your case, and use the abbreviated "table of contents" that follows to lead you through the relevant sections of the book.

I know nothing about investing or a 401(k) plan.

You'll find material of interest in every chapter, but if you're in a hurry, concentrate on the following chapters: **2**, "The 401(k) Plan: What It Is and How It Works"; **4**, "Should You Participate in Your Company's 401(k) Plan?"; **5**, "Using a 401(k) to Plan for Your Retirement"; **6**, "401(k) Investment

Strategies"; **13**, "Distributions and Loans from Your 401(k)"; and **Appendix A**, "Commonly Asked Questions."

I know nothing about investing or a 401(k) plan, but I have (or will soon be using) a qualified investment adviser.

Since your financial adviser should have a good under- standing of the pros and cons of different investments, but may not be overly familiar with the features of a 401(k), read the following chapters: **2**, "The 401(k) Plan: What It Is and How It Works"; **5**, "Using a 401(k) to Plan for Your Retirement"; **6**, "401(k) Investment Strategies"; **12**, "Life Insurance in Your 401(k)"; **13**, "Distributions and Loans from Your 401(k) Plan"; and **Appendix A**, "Commonly Asked Questions."

I have had a fair amount of experience when it comes to investing, however, I know nothing about the 401(k) plan offered through work.

The investor who has bought and sold some individual stocks and mutual funds should read the following chapters: **2**, "The 401(k) Plan: What It Is and How It Works"; **4**, "Should You Participate in Your Company's 401(k) Plan?"; **5**, "Using a 401(k) to Plan for Your Retirement"; **12**, "Life Insurance in Your 401(k)"; **13**, "Distributions and Loans from Your 401(k)"; and **Appendix A**, "Commonly Asked Questions."

I work closely with an investment adviser (or financial plan- ner). My adviser has already drafted a financial plan for me that includes retirement planning. The plan has been imple- mented, and, so far, I am content with the results. My compa- ny offers a 401(k), but my decision to participate will depend upon what my adviser tells me to do.

It appears that you are in good hands. Nevertheless, it is always valuable to look at investments from a new or different perspective. Spend an hour or so reading the following chapters: **4**, "Should You Participate in Your Company's 401(k) Plan?"; and **13**, "Distributions and Loans from Your 401(k)."

I believe I understand everything I need to know about my company's 401(k) plan, but I have no idea what investment options are best for me.

There are two areas you need to learn about, investments and financial planning. Read the following chapters: **5**, "Using a 401(k) to Plan for Your Retirement"; **6**, "401(k) Investment Strategies"; **8**, "Investing in Debt Instruments"; **9**, "Investing in Equity Instruments"; **10**, "Investing in Hybrids"; **11**, "Mutual Funds & Global Investing"; and **12**, "Life Insurance in Your 401(k)."

I know all I need to know about investments, life insurance, and qualified retirement plans, such as a 401(k). However, I would like to draft my own retirement plan.

You should be commended. Perhaps only 1-2 percent of the public has even a fair grasp of what investing is all about; even fewer are well versed when it comes to retirement plans. You only need to read the following chapters: **5**, "Using a 401(k) to Plan for Your Retirement"; **6**, "Investment Strategies"; and **Appendix A**, "Commonly Asked Questions."

I have a lump sum to invest (from a previous employer), and I am facing a deadline. I have to make some quick decisions as to which investments I should go into with this money.

Time is of the essence. You can learn more about financial planning and perhaps more about the workings of a 401(k) later. For now, selecting the right investments is your top priority. Read the following chapters: **6**, "401(k) Investment Strategies"; **8**, "Investing in Debt Instruments"; **9**, "Investing in Equity Instruments"; **10**, "Investing in Hybrids"; **11**, "Mutual Funds & Global Investing"; and **12**, "Life Insurance in Your 401(k)."

I am going to retire in five years (or less), and I am very worried about my future. I don't know what to expect, or even if it is too late to make some changes in my portfolio both inside and outside of my 401(k) account.

You may be a little late when it comes to comprehensive financial planning. (Although a good case can be made that it is never too late.) It sounds as if you either need some reassurance or a cold dose of reality. Read the following chapters: **5**, "Using a 401(k) to Plan for Your Retirement"; **6**, "401(k) Investment Strategies"; **8**, "Investing in Debt Instruments"; **9**, "Investing in Equity Instruments"; **11**, "Mutual Funds & Global Investing"; **12**, "Life Insurance in Your 401(k)"; **13**, "Distributions and Loans from Your 401(k) Plan"; and **Appendix A**, "Commonly Asked Questions."

No matter how inexperienced or knowledgeable you are, if, after reading parts or all of this book, you still feel you need some help, contact your employer and find out if your company has someone on site who is qualified to answer your questions about the 401(k) and investing. At large companies, this person may be referred to as the "employee benefits coordinator." Smaller firms may have a financial officer who is well versed about investments.

Whether your employer has such a resource or not, it is always useful to get a second opinion. There are several good sources you can turn to, but Certified Fund Specialists (CFS) is one of the better-trained groups of advisers. In order to earn the CFS designation, the adviser or broker must complete a comprehensive program that concentrates on the kinds of investments that are offered to you in a 401(k) plan. These professionals are also well equipped to provide you with general financial and retirement planning. For a list of Certified Fund Specialists in your area, telephone (800) 848-2029.

CHAPTER 2
The 401(k) Plan: What It Is and How It Works

This chapter is designed to help you quickly and easily understand what a 401(k) is and how it works, along with its advantages and disadvantages. It is made up of a series of brief, but critical entries explaining the key features. This format will also be useful if you use this book later as a reference and need to find information on a specific aspect of 401(k) plans.

A brief definition: A 401(k) is a type of retirement plan that is established by a company for the benefit of its workers. Contributions to the plan can be made by either the employee, the employer, or both. Workers who are covered by a 401(k) are called *participants*. A 401(k), just like a pension or profit-sharing plan, is a type of *qualified* retirement plan. Qualified retirement plans have certain tax advantages (see below).

401(k) plan requirements: A company cannot be required by its employees or anyone else to establish a 401(k) or any other kind of retirement plan. Subject to annual contribution limits, a company may offer more than one retirement plan to its employees. Workers are not required to participate in a company's 401(k) plan. Those who contribute into a 401(k), and/or have contributions made by the employer on their behalf, are not required to make a contribution for any given week, month, quarter, or year. In short, this is not the kind of retirement plan that is cast in stone. Just because a company or employee starts a 401(k) or decides to contribute to such a plan does not mean that the 401(k) must continue for a certain period of time or that the employee and/or employer is forced or required to make contributions for a set number of periods or years.

How the plan is structured: If you participate in a 401(k) plan, you have an account of your own. As the "owner" of the account, you decide how your contributions are to be invested, even if those contributions are made by your employer. Your investment alternatives are limited by the plan. You cannot force the company you work for to add or delete certain investments. You also have the right to periodically reposition your existing holdings. Again, any changes you make are limited by the plan's rules and limitations.

Your investment choices: Every 401(k) plan offers one or more investment choices or options. Most plans offer four to eight different selections, although some plans offer only a couple and others offer dozens of choices. Possible investment options range from the conservative, such as money market accounts, to the aggressive, such as individual stocks or a mutual fund that invests in what are referred to as small-company stocks.

The most likely investment choices: The typical 401(k) plan offers a money market fund, a growth fund, a balanced fund (stocks and bonds), and a government bond fund. If the company you work for has its own stock, then company stock is often offered as an option. As the participant and the owner of your account, you tell your employer—typically at the beginning of the quarter—if you want to change your allocation. For example, if $300 is taken out of every one of your paychecks (or your company is contributing $300), your might allocate these investment dollars as follows: 50 percent to a growth fund, 30 percent to a balanced fund, and 20 percent to company stock. At the beginning of the next quarter you could change your allocation, using different investments and different weightings—depending on changes in your investment strategies or goals.

Life insurance within 401(k)s: Some plans allow participants to purchase life insurance with 401(k) dollars. For most people, this is the only way to get life insurance with *pre-tax* dollars (since the contributions are deductible). There are limitations on how much life insurance can be purchased inside a 401(k) account. If the limits are exceeded, the participant will be taxed on a portion of the excess amount.

Annual contribution limits: There is a limit on how much can be contributed each year to a 401(k) account. The limit is 15 percent of your compensation or $9,240, whichever is less. Thus, if Mary Smith has an annual salary of $60,000, up to $9,000 can be contributed to her 401(k) account ($60,000 x 15 percent = $9,000). Contribution limits are the same whether the contributions are made by the employer, the employee, or both.

Inflation indexing: The maximum annual contribution, which is $9,500 for 1996, is indexed for inflation. This means that the maximum contribution should be increased for

1997, 1998, etc. The exact increase for upcoming years is
unknown, since any increase may or may not exactly reflect
the previous year's rate of inflation. (For example, the 1995
limit was the same as the 1994 limit, even though there was
inflation in 1994.)

No "making up" for lost time: As is true for almost all
retirement plans, a 401(k) does not allow the employee or
employer to "make up for lost time." The fact that you have
just recently joined the company's 401(k) plan, even if the
plan has been in place for a number of years, does not mean
that you or the company can increase or double up on contributions made on your behalf. Similarly, long-time employees
of a company that has just recently established a 401(k) cannot make extra contributions to make up for the years during
which a retirement plan was not offered.

What you are entitled to: Participants are always free to
withdraw all of their own contributions plus the earnings from
such contributions. This is not necessarily the case when it
comes to employer contributions and their respective earnings
or growth. Employer contributions may be subject to a *vesting*
schedule (for the definition of vesting, see below). This means
that the participant can withdraw only that portion (percentage) of the employer's contributions that have become vested.
The vesting schedule may last one or several years. Vesting
schedules are designed to encourage workers to stay with the
same employer for long periods of time. If a participant leaves
the company before he or she is fully vested, the portion of the
employer's contributions that is not vested is forfeited.

The vesting schedule: Employers have a certain degree
of flexibility when it comes to setting up a vesting schedule. As

an example, one employer's 401(k) plan may state that employees are 20 percent vested at the end of the first year, 40 percent vested at the end of the second year, 60 percent vested at the end of the third year, 80 percent vested at the end of the fourth year, and 100 percent vested at the end of the fifth year. Thus, if the employer's contributions, and the growth from such contributions, totaled $8,000 at the end of the third year, an employee would be entitled to withdraw up to 60 percent of that $8,000 if he or she left the company. A number of 401(k) plans have no vesting schedule, meaning that the employee is immediately entitled to 100 percent of any contributions (and their subsequent growth) made by the employer. By law, employees are always entitled to any contributions (plus any resulting growth or income) they have made on their own.

Notification of vesting: If your company offers you a 401(k), they must disclose whether or not there is a vesting schedule and, if so, how it works.

An example of vesting: John Smith works for the XYZ Company, which has a 401(k) plan. For every dollar John contributes, XYZ also contributes a dollar (this is referred to as a *matching program*). The 401(k) plan established by XYZ has a vesting schedule that states that an employee is 25 percent vested at the end of the first year and 100 percent vested at the end of the second year. Halfway through John's second year, he leaves to accept another job with a different company. Upon his termination, John learns that the $4,500 he has contributed has grown to $5,000, as has the $4,500 contributed by XYZ. However, since John stayed with XYZ for a little over a year, he is only 25 percent vested. Therefore, when John leaves XYZ, he may take with him the following amounts: (1) the $4,500 he contributed, (2) the $500 growth and income from his own contributions, (3) 25 percent of the $4,500 contributed by XYZ, and (4) 25 percent of the $500 of growth and income due to the XYZ contributions—for a total of $6,250. Had John stayed for two full years, he would have been entitled to the entire account balance of $10,000.

Tax consequences: Money invested in a 401(k) plan grows and compounds tax-deferred, but is not tax-free. This means that there is no tax liability as long as the money stays in a 401(k) or other qualified retirement plan. However, once money is taken out, it is fully taxable in the year in which it is received. As an example, suppose Jane has a 401(k) account that is worth $110,000. She is sixty-two years old and wants to take out $20,000. Jane can take out $20,000, but she must report $20,000 of additional income in the year in which the withdrawal is made.

Income averaging: When you retire, you may be able to take advantage of either five-year or ten-year income averaging to reduce the taxes on part or all of your withdrawals.

Employer contributions: Your employer can take contributions made on your behalf as a deduction (for income tax purposes). Your taxable income, however, is not increased or decreased.

Employee contributions: Typically, employee contributions are deducted from your paycheck. In most cases, your take-home pay will be less, but so will your taxable income. Your taxable income is lowered by the amount of your contribution.

Withdrawals: Money can be taken out of a 401(k) plan at any time. However, the employee is entitled only to his own contributions and that portion of the employer's contributions that are vested (see "vesting" above). Withdrawals can be made in specific cases: (1) retirement, (2) death, (3) disability, (4) termination of employment, (5) reaching age 59 1/2, (6) leaving the company after reaching age fifty-five or older, (7) changing jobs, (8) loans, (9) the company's terminating the plan, (10) "hardship" withdrawals, and (11) withdrawals made prior to retirement. The most common of these types of withdrawals is discussed below, along with any penalties or tax consequences.

Hardship withdrawals: One unique feature of 401(k) plans, compared to other qualified retirement plans, is that hardship withdrawals are permitted. The IRS requires that a hardship withdrawal meets two criteria: (1) The employee has immediate and substantial financial needs, and (2) money is not available from other sources to meet such a financial crisis. The "immediate and substantial" part of the test can be satisfied if the money being withdrawn is used: (1) for medical expenses incurred by the participant, the participant's spouse, or the participant's dependents, (2) for purchase of a principal residence, (3) for tuition payments for the next twelve months of postsecondary education for the participant or the participant's spouse or dependents, or (4) to prevent eviction of the participant from his or her home or the foreclosure of a mortgage on the home. The second criterion, the lack of other sources of funds, is determined by the participant's personal circumstances.

Loans: Some 401(k) plans allow participants to take money out, free of any IRS penalty or income taxes, through loans. In essence, the participant is borrowing money from himself or herself. And, just as when you borrow money from a bank, there are no income tax consequences. Even though you are borrowing money from yourself, you must still pay yourself back—with interest. Ordinarily, the interest rate on these loans is approximately the prime rate. The interest and principal payments (all loans must be amortized) go directly back into your account. Unless the loan is used to purchase a primary residence, it must be fully paid back within five years. Because of the additional expenses of administering this kind of program, most 401(k) plans do not offer a loan provision.

Penalty for early withdrawals: The IRS imposes a 10 percent penalty on 401(k) plan withdrawals, *except* for distributions (1) after age 59 1/2, (2) due to the employee's death, (3) due to the employee's disability, (4) that are part of a lifetime annuity payout following termination of employment, (5) to an employee who is fifty-five or older and has terminated employment, or (6) for medical expenses. Participants who make withdrawals under one of these exceptions must still pay income taxes on the amount(s) taken out.

Rollovers: If you leave your current employer and go to work for another company, you can transfer your 401(k) account into your new employer's 401(k) plan. If the new company you are going to work for does not have a 401(k), you may roll the money into an IRA account. You can also roll the money into your own IRA even if your new boss has a 401(k) (you may not like the investment choices the plan offers). The key to a successful rollover is to make sure that the check (representing your vested interest in the account) is not made out to you, and that you do not take receipt of any money. A "direct" rollover to a new plan—a transfer directly between your former plan and a new one, or into an IRA you've set up at a bank, brokerage firm, mutual fund, or insurance company—avoids taxes and the 10 percent IRS penalty.

Advantages: The reasons why you should strongly consider participating in your company's 401(k) plan include the following: (1) Some part, or all, of the contributions may be made by your employer (these contributions cost you nothing), (2) all administrative costs are usually paid by the employer, not the employee (no matter who makes the contributions), (3) money in 401(k) plans grows and compounds faster because it is not subject to income taxes each year, (4) the plan may offer a number of investment choices that you find appealing, (5) some plans allow employees to take out tax-free loans, (6) hardship withdrawals are allowed under certain circumstances, (7) money can be taken out penalty-free in the event of death or disability, and (8) special income averaging advantages are available at retirement.

Disadvantages: There are a few reasons why you may not want to be part of a 401(k): (1) There is no guarantee that you will have enough money in your 401(k) or any other qualified plan to maintain your standard of living when you retire, (2) some other retirement plans have annual contribution limits that are higher than those under a 401(k), (3) you may not be happy with some or all of the investment choices you are offered, and (4) you bear the risk and reward when it comes to the account's performance—like most retirement plans, a 401(k) cannot, in advance, promise to pay you a set number of dollars per month when you retire.

This chapter has highlighted the important aspects of a 401(k), including the pros and cons of participating in this kind of retirement plan. The next chapter will discuss how 401(k)s compare to some other common retirement plans. The information will be helpful to you if (1) you have the ability to participate in more than one *kind* of retirement plan, (2) you are about to leave an employer that has one type of retirement plan and your new employer has a different kind of plan, (3) you already have a retirement plan that you are familiar with, such as an IRA, and would like to see how it compares with a 401(k), or (4) you, or you and your spouse, are contributing to different kinds of plans and you would like to determine how future contributions should be allocated.

CHAPTER 3
401(k)s Compared to Other Retirement Plans

The first pension plans for workers were started in Prussia during the 1860s. Bismarck is credited with selecting age 65 as the official age of retirement. At that time, few workers lived long enough to reach retirement age. According to the U.S. National Center for Health Statistics, life expectancy in 1900 was 46 years old. It was not until the late 1940s that life expectancy in the United States reached 65 years.

American Express was the first U.S. company to set up an employer-sponsored retirement plan. Five years later, in 1880, the Baltimore and Ohio Railroad became the second. By the early part of the twentieth century, pensions covered less than 10 percent of the private sector. By the end of the 1930s, there were fewer than six hundred employer-sponsored retirement plans in the country. However, one year after the end of World War II, there were more than seven thousand such plans, covering three million workers.

After the 1935 passage of the Social Security and Railroad Retirement Systems Act, the next big development in retirement programs came in 1962, when Congress passed HR-10, allowing people who were self-employed to have tax-advantaged retirement plans (also referred to as Keogh plans). Ten years later, in 1972, the Employee Retirement Income Security Act (ERISA) was passed. ERISA created IRA accounts along with the Pension Benefit Guaranty Corporation, which to this day insures the benefits promised by corporations that provide defined-benefit retirement plans. 401(k) plans were authorized by the Retirement Act of 1978, but it was not until the end of 1981 that the IRS decided that employees could make tax-deductible contributions—which led to a tremendous growth of interest in the plans.

A QUICK PROFILE OF THE 401(K) PLAN

A quick review of the statistics about how American companies and workers use 401(k)s will give you some idea of how important these plans have become.

Today, close to $3 trillion is invested in private pension assets (e.g., defined-benefit plans, Keoghs, profit-sharing plans, etc.); of that, a little over $500 billion is invested in 401(k) plans alone. Based on current growth rates, it is projected that this figure will easily top the $1 trillion mark by the end of the century.

Only about 40 percent of American businesses have any kind of retirement plan. The figures are the same for the 750,000 new companies that are started each year in this country. In fact, only about 10 percent of the 1.7 million companies with between five and fifty employees had a 401(k) plan by the end of 1994. In all, close to a quarter of a million corporations offer a 401(k) plan.

Seventy-five percent of the twenty-five million employees who are eligible to participate in 401(k)s do so. Brokerage firm studies indicate that only about a third of those who participate end up investing the maximum amount allowed. This is almost a crime when you consider that this means most employees do not take full advantage of the matching contributions made by their employer.

Almost 85 percent of all companies that have 401(k) plans make contributions on behalf of their employees. Of these companies, 7 percent make contributions even if the employees do not. The typical employer contribution to a 401(k) plan is around $800 per participant (employee) per year, and the average employee contribution is $1,600. A 1994 survey by *Worth* magazine found that a few companies contributed as much as 2-3 dollars for every dollar contributed by the employee. Other companies made no matching contributions at all. Of those that did match, the most frequent type of matching was dollar for dollar, up to 6 percent of the employee's salary.

Almost two-thirds of the companies that have a 401(k) pay for all plan expenses. The remaining one-third is evenly split on how they pay for the administration of their plan: Half split the costs with the participants (the employees in the plan), and half charge all expenses to the participants.

The number of investment choices (i.e., a growth portfolio, a balanced fund comprised of stocks and bonds, foreign securities, etc.) for 401(k) plan participants now averages between five and six. About 30 percent of the companies that have a 401(k) allow employees to make investment changes daily; close to 90 percent of the employers that provide these plans allow changes or transfers at least quarterly. Plan participants make all investment decisions in 80 percent of the outstanding 401(k) programs.

The average employee has $16,000 in his or her 401(k) account. Distribution of 401(k) assets by type of investment is as follows: guaranteed rate of return, 30 percent; common stocks, 30 percent; company stock, 15 percent; government and corporate bonds, 10 percent; balanced funds, 6 percent; and money market accounts, 5 percent.

With these statistics in mind, it's important to look at just how 401(k) plans compare to the other qualified retirement investment programs that you may encounter.

401(K) BENEFITS

The greatest appeal of a 401(k) plan, as compared to other kinds of plans that companies can set up, is its flexibility. The employee decides how much to contribute to his account each quarter and how the money is invested (e.g., money market, company stock, a growth portfolio, bond account, etc.). In even the most basic plans, employees typically have a minimum of four choices: a money market account, a growth fund, a growth and income fund, and government bonds. A number of plans now also offer foreign equities, global bonds, high-yield bonds, and aggressive growth stocks. The employer is free to change plans at any time in order to limit or expand the employees' investment choices.

Contributions can be made in a number of different ways. They can be deducted from an employee's salary, the employer can make all contributions, or the plan can be set up so that a specific dollar amount or set percentage of the employee's compensation is contributed by the company—and any additional amount to be contributed by the employee.

Speaking of contributions, some mutual fund families that normally charge a sales fee (which would be deducted from each of your contributions) will waive such charges for 401(k) investments—depending on the size of the plan.

The 401(k) plan also offers significant tax benefits. Besides getting a tax deduction for contributions, and the potential for tax-deferred growth (both discussed in the chapter that follows), you may qualify for special tax treatment if you withdraw your 401(k) money all at once when you retire. Known as "forward averaging" or "income averaging," this allows you to pay taxes on the lump sum as if the withdrawals had been made over five years (10 years for some participants), rather than in just one year. For most people, this will result in lower taxes.

Other benefits of 401(k)s include portability—and the way they encourage disciplined investing. You can transfer your 401(k) account to your next employer or into an IRA without paying any taxes or IRS penalties. The money you transfer includes all of the contributions you made plus any contributions made by your employer that are vested, plus the growth and interest from such investments. "Investment discipline" may sound boring, but it shouldn't. Most people lack the discipline to invest even small amounts of money on a regular basis. Once you begin participating in a 401(k), payroll deductions become automatic, making investment a less "painful" experience (since you do not have to write out a check once or twice a month).

There *are* disadvantages to 401(k) plans. First, money taken out before age 59 1/2 is usually subject to income taxes *and* a 10 percent IRS penalty. Second, you may not like the investment choices you have within the 401(k)—they may be either too conservative or too aggressive for you.

Let's look at how the 401(k) compares to other retirement programs. As an employee, you may be able to set up or participate in one or more of these other programs, even if you make contributions to a 401(k) plan. The following plans will be examined: (1) IRAs, (2) Keoghs, (3) annuities, (4) money purchase pension plans, and (5) SEPs.

IRAS

Individual retirement accounts (IRAs) were created in 1974. Legislation passed in 1981 greatly broadened eligibility for IRA accounts. However, the 1986 Tax Reform Act limited the number of people who could benefit from this kind of account.

In order to be eligible for an IRA, you must meet two tests: (1) you must have earned income and (2) be under age 70 1/2. "Earned income" is money you receive from your salary, tips, bonuses, or commissions. "Unearned income" represents income from sources such as your investments and includes things such as interest, capital gains, and rent. Money from income-producing property may be classified as "earned" income, depending upon how much of your time is spent managing or overseeing the property. Individuals who are past age 70 1/2 may keep their IRA account(s), but they can't set up another IRA or make additional contributions to existing ones.

If you are eligible, you may contribute up to $2,000 per year. If your spouse works, he or she may also contribute up to $2,000 each year—to their own account. You cannot set up a joint IRA account with your spouse—or anyone else. Whether or not your spouse works, each person must have a separate account.

The limit on your contributions increases to $2,250 if your spouse is not working. You can split the contribution any way you wish, but your contribution to either account cannot be greater than $2,000. This means that if your spouse does not work, you could contribute up to $2,250 and divide it as follows: (1) $2,000 in your IRA, $250 in your spouse's; (2) $2,000 in the nonworking spouse's account, $250 in your own; (3) $1,125 in each account; or (4) any other combination you can think of that adds up to $2,250, as long as neither is greater than $2,000. If your spouse also works, you may contribute up to a total of $4,000, provided, again, that neither of you receives more than $2,000 worth of contributions in his or her account for that year. A working spouse may also elect to be treated, for IRA purposes, as having no compensation—electing to have contributions made under the spousal IRA provisions.

Unlike other kinds of retirement plans, you do not have to rely on your employer to set up and fund an IRA. Whether or not your company has one or more other retirement plans is not important. Whether or not your IRA contribution is deductible will depend upon your level of compensation and whether you are a participant in a company plan.

You can have an IRA no matter how much money you and your spouse earn. Even if one or both of you make millions a year, you can still set up or fund an IRA, provided you meet the two tests described above. Individuals or couples who make lots of money can fully deduct their IRA contribution(s), provided that neither spouse participates in another retirement plan. If you or your spouse is part of another plan, whether or not your contributions are deductible depends upon your adjusted gross income (AGI).

Most people do not realize that where the money to fund an IRA comes from is not important, as long as you have *earned* income. This means that you could end up spending all of your salary, leaving no money left to invest in an IRA, but still make the contribution by having someone make a gift to you, obtaining a loan, or liquidating part of an existing investment.

Since the IRS is not concerned with where the money comes from, you can make sure that IRA contributions are made each year, as long as you have a source to tap (e.g., a commercial bank, a loan from mom and dad, a gift from the grandparents, interest or dividends from an investment, or the sale proceeds from anything). This can be an important feature in a retirement investment—where regular saving and investing is critical.

IRA money can be invested in anything but the following:

(1) collectibles such as rare coins or stamps, (2) bullion, (3) commodities (futures contracts), (4) options (except what is referred to as "covered call writing"), and (5) anything that is considered self-dealing (e.g., you cannot invest in your own real estate or any other form of real estate, oil well, or leasing program, unless you are a limited partner within a limited partnership).

Generally, money taken out of an IRA prior to the participant's reaching age 59 1/2 is subject to a 10 percent penalty and ordinary income taxes. Partial liquidations or full redemptions made prior to age 59 1/2 are not subject to the 10 percent IRS penalty if the account owner is considered to be permanently disabled or dies. The only other way to take money out of an IRA if you are under 59 1/2 without a penalty is if the distributions are based on life expectancy. This means that if a 40-year-old has a remaining life expectancy of forty-five more years, he or she could take out 1/45 of the account value, each year, without penalty. All withdrawals are still subject to ordinary income taxes, whether the recipient is the original owner or an heir. Once you reach age 59 1/2, withdrawals can be made for whatever reason without penalty.

Unlike 401(k) plans, you can not take money out of an IRA for hardship cases. The maximum contribution limits for IRAs are also significantly lower than for 401(k) plans. Finally, the potential for using income-averaging techniques to lower your tax exposure on withdrawal —available for 401(k)s—is not available for IRA accounts.

KEOGH PLANS

Keogh plans are for people who are self-employed or who work for a company that is not incorporated. Like other kinds of retirement plans, Keoghs are designed to help people accumulate a nest egg for their later years. As in a 401(k) or IRA, investments in a Keogh grow and compound tax-deferred; only the moneys withdrawn are taxable.

In order to be eligible for a Keogh, you must have earned income that is derived from your own business. You may also be eligible if your employer has such a plan. (Only companies that are not incorporated may set up Keogh plans.) If you have your own business you are eligible to set up a Keogh, even if you are covered under an employer's retirement plan. As with a 401(k) plan, you can not force your employer to establish this, or any other, type of retirement account.

The maximum annual contribution to a Keogh is the lesser of 25 percent of *net* earned income (defined as compensation from the unincorporated business minus all business expenses including the Keogh contribution) or $30,000. Whether or not a minimum investment is required each year depends upon the type of plan you have. As with an IRA, the actual contribution can come from any source (e.g., a check from your grandparents or a loan from a bank). The IRS does not care where the money comes from, as long as your contributions follow the rules for Keogh plans.

Keogh plans come in three different versions: (1) defined-contribution, (2) defined-benefit, and (3) profit-sharing plans.

A defined-contribution plan, as the name implies, means that the annual *investment* is known or defined up front. The figure can range up to 25 percent of net earnings. Once you've chosen the annual contribution, it cannot be adjusted upward or downward. This is one of the few retirement plans that forces you to make a contribution each year.

A defined-benefit plan means that you've established a target retirement *benefit* in advance. The maximum annual retirement benefit must be less than 100 percent of the average of your three highest years of preretirement self-employment earnings or $120,000 (this figure is indexed for inflation and therefore is expected to be higher in the future). A defined-benefit plan is more expensive to establish and administer because it is more complicated than other plans and requires the use of an actuary each year. For younger people, the maximum allowable contributions are often lower than those for the other kinds of Keogh plans since they have more time to make contributions and there should be greater compounding. For people in their fifties or older, maximum contributions may easily exceed the $30,000 annual limit imposed by other plans.

The final Keogh option, a profit-sharing plan, allows you to contribute up to 15 percent of your income each year. This figure can vary *each* year from 0 to 15 percent. Total contributions for any year cannot exceed $30,000. The relatively low maximum percentage figure used to determine the contribution is a disadvantage. A defined-contribution plan, by comparison, is allowed to use any figure up to 25 percent of net income.

In order to gain the maximum flexibility for contribution and discretion, a number of people have what is sometimes referred to as a "hybrid" or "combination" plan. What this means is that they have established *both* a profit-sharing plan and a defined-contribution plan. By setting the defined-contribution plan at 10 percent and the profit-sharing plan at 15 percent of net compensation, the maximum percentage figure of 25 percent can still be reached and a certain amount of flexibility is maintained.

Keogh accounts can be established through the same sources as IRA accounts (banks, savings and loan associations, brokerage firms, insurance companies, and mutual fund companies) and can contain the same instruments as 401(k)s and IRAs. The same restrictions on self-dealing are applicable to Keoghs.

Withdrawals are subject to ordinary income taxes. Money taken out of a Keogh prior to age 59 1/2 is also subject to a 10 percent penalty. There are several ways to avoid this penalty: (1) disability, (2) separation from service after age 55 with withdrawals made each year based on one's life expectancy (or joint lives if the worker is married), (3) to pay for certain medical expenses, or (4) to reduce excess contributions that were originally made by mistake.

If you are an *employee* and you participate in a Keogh, you can borrow money from your account for up to five years— longer if the money is used to purchase a primary residence. Unlike with a 401(k) plan, you do not have to show hardship. Like the 401(k), the money must be paid back with interest. When it comes to Keogh-related loans, the Internal Revenue Code discriminates against employers. If you are your own boss (i.e., a 5 percent or greater owner of a company or an independent contractor), you cannot borrow money from your Keogh for any reason. Any such attempted transactions are considered ordinary withdrawals, triggering the 10 percent penalty on top of ordinary income taxes.

Compared to 401(k) participants, Keogh plan participants have the potential to contribute much more money each year. However, if you work for a company that has a Keogh, only the employer can make a contribution on your behalf, and the contribution cannot lower your existing salary or compensation. Since the burden falls completely on the company and not the employee, it is much less likely that a company will set up a Keogh instead of a 401(k) plan.

ANNUITIES

Within the financial services community, an *annuity* is defined as a contractual relationship between the investor and an insurance company. There are two types of annuities, fixed-rate and variable. A fixed-rate annuity is similar to a bank CD; the investor is guaranteed a set rate of return for a specific period of time. A variable annuity is similar to a mutual fund family; the investor can invest money in one or more of the portfolios within the annuity "family."

An annuity is not a type of retirement plan, but instead a type of investment that can be purchased either inside or outside a retirement plan. When an annuity is purchased outside a plan, as a regular investment, you cannot take a deduction. Only when an annuity is part of a qualified retirement plan, such as a 401(k), Keogh, IRA, or profit-sharing plan, may the contribution end up being tax-deductible. Our discussion will focus on annuities as they are used *outside*—or as an alternative to—a qualified retirement plan. As you will see, using an annuity for nonretirement money can still be an effective way to postpone income taxes indefinitely.

There are four parties to every annuity: (1) the contract owner, sometimes referred to as the investor, (2) the annuitant, (3) the beneficiary, and (4) the insurer. In order to minimize confusion, a brief description of each party is warranted.

The *contract owner* is almost always the person who makes the investment. (Technically, the investment is called the contract.) The contract owner decides where the money will be invested and also names the annuitant and the beneficiary. As when shopping for a certificate of deposit or mutual fund, the contract owner can deal with any insurance company that offers annuities. The contract owner can be an individual (some companies allow both spouses to be owners), a trust, a charity, or a business.

The *annuitant* is what is referred to as the "measuring life." The annuity investment can stay in place as long as the contract owner likes or until the annuitant dies, whichever occurs first. The annuitant serves no other purpose. The annuitant is not entitled to any of the money in the account and has no say as to ownership or who is named as the beneficiary. The annuitant must be an individual; you cannot name a trust, partnership, couple, or charity as the annuitant. Insurance companies typically require that the annuitant be under age 75.

The *beneficiary* receives the value of the contract (the investment) upon the death of the annuitant. The beneficiary can be changed at any time without his or her knowledge or consent. The beneficiary has no rights in an annuity until the annuitant dies. The beneficiary can be an individual, couple, children, friend, relative, trust, estate, partnership, company, or charity.

The *insurer* is the company that offers the annuity. All annuities, both fixed-rate and variable, are offered by the insurance industry. It is the insurer that determines what products it will offer. The rates and terms offered can vary quite a bit from insurer to insurer, just as CD rates vary from one bank to another.

Virtually anyone can have an annuity. Even a minor child can own an annuity (such an account would be titled, "John Jones, Sr., custodian for the benefit of John Jones, Jr."). Furthermore, there are no maximum contribution limits. Since you do not get a deduction for investing in an annuity, the IRS does not care how much money you invest. Most insurance companies that offer annuities have a $1,000 or $5,000 minimum (lower if the annuity is part of a qualified retirement plan such as an IRA or Keogh).

Although contributions are not deductible, money in an annuity grows and compounds tax-deferred until it is withdrawn. Money can come from any source. Most *variable* annuity contracts allow you to make additional contributions at any time. Money usually cannot be added to a fixed-rate annuity (just as it normally cannot be added to a bank CD); however, if there is additional money to invest, a second, third, or fourth annuity can be purchased from the same or a different company. You are never required to add money to any *nonqualified* annuity.

Money taken out of any annuity prior to the contract owner's reaching age 59 1/2 is subject to a 10 percent IRS penalty—as money prematurely taken out of an IRA would be. And, just as with an IRA or Keogh, the 10 percent IRS penalty can be avoided by death, disability, or withdrawals based on the contract owner's life expectancy (e.g., if your life expectancy was thirty years, one-thirtieth of the account could be liquidated each year without penalty). If the fixed-rate or variable annuity is annuitized (described below) within the first year, the pre-59 1/2 penalty is also waived.

Annuitization is the process of withdrawing money over a specific number of years or based on someone's life expectancy. Substantially even distributions are made annually; the checks can be received either monthly, quarterly, semiannually, or annually. The amount of each distribution depends upon the time period selected, the value of the account, and how well the portfolio is performing.

Because of the pre-59 1/2 IRS penalty of 10 percent, annuities are best suited for individuals and couples who are willing to tie their money up until they reach at least 59 1/2. Tax-deferred growth is a powerful investment tool, but a 10 percent IRS penalty could erode part or all of the potential tax savings.

Comparing annuities to 401(k) plans is not particularly straightforward, since a 401(k) plan participant can select an annuity as an investment if it is offered by his plan. Comparing *nonqualified* annuities with 401(k) plans is much easier.

First, you do not get a tax deduction for contributions to a nonqualified annuity.

Second, the IRS still imposes a penalty for pre-59 1/2 withdrawals. Taking out your principal contribution(s), however, is not a taxable event. Thus, if you invested $20,000 in a nonqualified fixed-rate or variable annuity and it grew to $28,000, only the first $8,000 withdrawn would be taxable.

Third, the great majority of annuities include a back-end charge that lapses after a certain number of years. Typically, you can withdraw up to 10 percent *each year* without cost, fee, or penalty. Any excess withdrawals made during the penalty period, which usually lasts seven years, are subject to a penalty in the 5-7 percent range. Once the penalty period expires, partial withdrawals or complete liquidations can be made without any insurance company charge.

Millions of people use nonqualified annuities because they are looking for ways to shelter their income from current taxation, and either cannot participate in a retirement plan or have already contributed their maximum allowable amount to a qualified plan.

MONEY-PURCHASE PENSION PLANS

A money-purchase pension is yet another kind of qualified retirement plan. The company must be incorporated to have such a plan; unincorporated businesses can have a similar plan, but such plans are governed by the rules of Keogh accounts. Each employee has an individual account. Contributions can be made only by the employer, and cannot lower the employee's compensation.

Once a money-purchase plan has been established, all employees are eligible to participate in the program. The employer can exclude only those employees who have less than one year of service, are under age 21, or work less than five hundred hours per year. Once an employee satisfies all three hurdles (time of service, age, and hours per year), he or she must be included in future contributions.

Employer contributions cannot exceed 25 percent of an employee's annual compensation or $30,000, whichever is less. Since there is almost always a difference in compensation from one employee to another, this means that different dollar amounts will be contributed for different employees. All employer contributions are tax-deductible to the company.

A few money-purchase pension plans allow after-tax contributions by employees. Since these contributions would be made with after-tax dollars, the employee would not receive a deduction, but their contributions would still enjoy tax-deferred growth.

Participants in a money-purchase plan have the same flexibility that investors in other plans have: You are limited only by the investments offered by the plan's sponsor (a mutual fund group, insurance company, or brokerage firm). As with a 401(k) plan, you may have the option, with lump-sum distributions after age 59 1/2, of using a special five-year averaging income tax calculation; a few older participants may be eligible for ten-year averaging.

SEPS

SEPs (for Simplified Employee Pension) represent another type of employer-sponsored retirement plan. Sometimes referred to as "SEP-IRAs," a SEP is like IRAs, but with three big differences: (1) The employer makes the contribution, (2) the upper limits are much higher, and (3) the contributions cannot be discriminatory. Even though SEPs are considered a type of IRA, they are distinct from IRAs for contribution purposes. That is, an individual could contribute the maximum to his or her own IRA and still contribute the maximum to a SEP.

The annual limits for SEP contributions are 15 percent of the employee's compensation or $30,000, whichever is less. Thus, the guidelines and restrictions are identical to those of profit-sharing plans. A SEP can be funded through salary reductions (meaning that the employee has less take-home pay) or by the employer. Contributions are deductible by whichever party makes the investment.

A great benefit to the employer is that SEP contributions do not have to be made every year. This means that the company can omit making contributions on behalf of employees for as many years in a row as it likes.

Unlike those from 401(k) plans, distributions from SEPs are not eligible for either five or ten-year income tax averaging. SEP plans can also be set up so that employee contributions are allowed. These plans, formally known as SARSEPs, allow an employer to set up a qualified retirement plan without having to make any direct contribution on behalf of employees, just like the flexibility allowed under 401(k) plans.

Compared to these other plans, the 401(k) offers a broad range of distinct advantages—from the flexibility it offers in how contributions are made, the deductibility of the contributions, and the great variety of investment choices if offers, to the tax advantages income-averaging offers on withdrawals. But as with all retirement investments, the 401(k) plan is only a good choice for you if the plan your company offers fits your investment goals. The next chapter will look at how you can decide whether your employer's 401(k) is the right place to put your investment dollars.

CHAPTER 4

Should You Participate in Your Company's 401(k) Plan?

Let us suppose that the company you are working for is about to establish a 401(k) or already has one in place. You are contacted and asked whether or not you want to participate in the plan. Since participation in a 401(k) is completely voluntary and no one can force you to join, the decision to be included in or excluded from the plan is yours and yours alone.

Deciding whether or not you should participate in a 401(k) plan should be based on the following: (1) whether your employer will contribute to the plan, (2) your tax bracket, (3) the investment selections available as part of the plan, (4) the caliber of the portfolio manager, and (5) your plans for retirement.

EMPLOYER CONTRIBUTIONS

Whether or not to participate in a 401(k) plan is a no-brainer if the boss is making the contributions on your behalf. You cannot lose. No matter how poorly the investments fare or how little is being contributed on your behalf, you will still always be better off. Why? Because nothing came out of your pocket, the contributions made on your behalf are not counted as income until they are withdrawn, and even if the contributions are small, a few hundred or thousand dollars is better than nothing.

For the great majority of prospective participants, the decision is not so easy. Most 401(k) plans are structured so that the employer pays either only a portion of what the participant contributes or nothing at all. Suppose the company puts in only 10 percent of every dollar contributed—meaning that ninety cents of every dollar comes out of your pocket. In most cases, even this minor contribution makes the 401(k) a good deal. If the investment you select just breaks even for the first year, your ninety cents will still "grow" to one dollar—based on your employer's contributions alone. You'll be making an 11 percent return on your investment without taking any risk (ten cents divided by ninety cents).

If your company does not make contributions on behalf of its employees, your decision will require more analysis. In this case, the other factors discussed above, your tax situation, the available investment choices, and quality of management, along with your overall financial situation, become the determining factors. Therefore, for the balance of this brief chapter, let's assume that you'll have to make any 401(k) contributions yourself, and see how these other factors come into play.

YOUR TAX BRACKET

The higher your tax bracket, the more tax benefits a qualified retirement plan—like a 401(k)—offers. For example, someone in the lowest tax bracket (at this point, 15 percent) reduces his or her taxable income by $15 for every $100 he contributes to a qualified plan. This is certainly beneficial, but if you are in the 33 percent bracket, Uncle Sam contributes $33 of every $100 you put into a 401(k) plan. (Since the con-

tributions are made in pretax dollars, the $100 you contribute
to a qualified plan would only be $67 if you contributed it to a
retirement plan on an after-tax basis.)

It gets even better. The tax benefits increase once you
include *state* income taxes. Almost every state now has a personal income tax. Since each state has different tax brackets
and treats the deductibility of qualified retirement plans differently, the additional tax benefit depends upon the state you
live in.

You get an even greater long-term benefit through sheltering your investment income. If you invest money outside a
qualified plan, you have to pay taxes on the interest, dividends
or gains received each year. Outside of a qualified retirement
plan, the only way to get around these taxes is to invest in
Series EE bonds (issued by the U.S. government and purchased at banks), municipal bonds, whole life insurance, or
annuities. But there are limitations to each of these investments. Let's look quickly at these alternatives to see how they
compare to the 401(k).

Series EE Bonds

Series EE bonds are purchased for one-half of face value
and, if held until maturity, can be cashed in for full face value
or exchanged for new HH bonds. No taxes are due on the
accumulating value until the bonds are cashed in. However,
when an EE bond is cashed in, taxes are due on the difference
between the purchase price and the redemption price. (The
IRS does allow you to pay taxes on the interest each year as it
accumulates, but this would be a poor choice for most people.) There is really no way around this tax event. If you
exchange the EE bond(s) for HH bond(s), you've only postponed the taxation. HH bonds pay interest twice a year, and
the interest is fully taxable on your federal income tax return.

Series EE bonds do provide a guaranteed rate of return, and principal is always guaranteed. However, once you factor in the effects of inflation and (the eventual) taxation, the real annual rate of growth drops to the zero to 1 percent range. In fact, during high-inflation years, the *real* rate of return on Series EE bonds (the quoted rate minus inflation and taxes) is a *negative* number—meaning that you are actually losing either present or future purchasing power.

Municipal Bonds

Some people consider municipal bonds a tax-advantaged investment that offers an alternative to a qualified retirement plan such as a 401(k). Unlike interest on EE bonds, the interest from municipal bonds is tax-free, not tax-deferred. However, only the interest from municipal bonds is tax-free. If the bonds are ever sold or redeemed, the difference between the purchase price and the net proceeds is taxable if there is a profit or gain.

Although municipal bonds, unlike Series EE and HH bonds, are not backed by the full faith and credit of the U.S. government, well over 95 percent of all tax-free bonds are very safe. However, municipal bonds are subject to market value fluctuations, just like government and corporate bonds. (Series EE and HH bonds have no such market risk.)

When interest rates go up (or are expected to go up), the value of a bond drops. When rates either decline or are expected to decline, bonds go up in value. This means that even though certain types of bonds are considered to be conservative, fluctuations of value can, and do, take place almost daily. These changes in value may cause you to think twice about investing in intermediate- (five to fifteen years maturity) or long-term (remaining maturity of fifteen to thirty years) bonds, even those backed by the federal government. During

1994, for example, long-term U.S. government bonds declined in value by more than 12 percent; intermediate-term government bonds dropped by about 5 percent.

Whole Life Insurance & Annuities

Buying whole life insurance is another way to shelter money from taxes. If you, or another family member, really needs life insurance, it can be a good investment, depending on the policy's rate of return. Buying it for its tax benefits alone, however, is not a smart idea—this idea is covered in greater depth in chapter 12.

Insurance companies also offer annuities. These are more like EE bonds in that taxes are deferred, not eliminated, on any accumulated value. Accumulated growth or interest in an annuity is eventually taxed to either the owner of the contract or his or her heir(s). And, unlike life insurance, annuities do not allow tax-free loans.

These last few paragraphs have described the *tax-advantaged alternatives* to qualified retirement plans such as 401(k)s. Many of these investments could also be offered as part of a 401(k) plan, although in most cases there are better investments. Now let's see how the 401(k) plan compares to these alternatives for sheltering growth.

YOUR INVESTMENT CHOICES

Listed below are all of the investments that are possible in a 401(k). Your choices will be limited by the plan document for your 401(k)—and perhaps by the employer or the investment company that oversees the administration and management of the plan.

> aggressive growth mutual funds
> balanced funds (stocks and bonds)

bank CDs (0–10 year maturities)
corporate bond funds
covered call options
currently minted U.S. gold and silver coins
equity-income funds
fixed-rate annuities (0–10 year maturities)
foreign stock funds
global bond funds (U.S. and foreign)
government bond funds
government securities
growth and income funds
growth funds
high-yield bond funds
income funds
individual bonds
individual stocks
international bond funds
limited partnerships
metals funds
money market funds
real estate investment trusts (REITs)
sector funds (e.g., health care, high tech)
utility funds

Obviously, the options available to you, as well as the choices you make from those options, are critical to your long-term success and should be an important factor in deciding whether to participate or not.

Some investment management teams are more aggressive or more conservative than others. Since it's your money that's being invested, and your retirement that is at stake, it is important that you find an investment that fits your goals and tolerance of risk.

Obviously, when you invest in stock or bond funds, or your company's stock (if this option is available to you), there's no guarantee that your investment will grow. In fact, over time, it is almost guaranteed that an individual stock or an equity fund will have a losing year. When the prospectus or sales brochure states, "Past results are no guarantee of future results"—believe it!

However, even though stocks and certain categories of bonds can experience losses, these types of investments have—historically—outperformed less risky choices such as bank CDs, money market accounts, or guaranteed accounts. If you are patient, and can stick it out through the down periods, these are better long-term investments.

Although it may be difficult to believe, the investment categories you select make far more difference than who is managing the portfolio. In fact, over the long term, your choice of investment category (e.g., choosing between growth-oriented, growth and income, international stock, global bond funds, etc.) will probably determine over 90 percent of your investment results. The choice of portfolio manager (e.g., Mary Smith, John Doe, the XYZ Variable Annuity Co., or the ABC Mutual Fund Group) will probably determine less than 10 percent of your overall, long-term results.

It is more than likely that your plan will include at least a couple of good investment options that are managed by a qualified portfolio manager or management team. More detailed explanations of how to evaluate which investments are best for your 401(k) plan—as well as which to avoid—appear in the chapters that follow. In most cases, though, it's a question of which option to choose, not whether to participate.

YOUR PLANS FOR RETIREMENT

Finally, you need to consider your retirement plans. If you and your spouse are among the lucky people who can count on a rich relative to leave you a couple of million dollars, planning for your retirement may seem unnecessary. However, if you're like most people, you need to start planning *today!*

In reviewing your plans for retirement, you should consider: (1) you and your spouse's life expectancies, (2) how much money you'll need to cover your monthly expenses when you retire, (3) whether you or your spouse have other qualified retirement accounts, (4) whether you have other sources of income or investments that can be used during your retirement years, (5) your expectations for inflation over the years until you're ready to retire, and (6) whether you can count on Social Security to be around when you need it.

All of these factors, fairly evaluated, should give you the motivation to get started now on planning for your retirement. And, as shown in the examples above, it is difficult to do better than a 401(k) plan for building retirement savings.

CHAPTER 5

Using a 401(k) to Plan for Your Retirement

Few of us lived through the Great Depression, but as things stand now, it would have been great preparation for what our retirement is likely to be like. A 1993 study found that nearly eight out of ten Americans will have less than half the income they need to retire comfortably. Unfortunately, the declining number of workers supporting the Social Security system and the continuing shift from traditional corporate pensions to employee-directed and funded retirement plans has transferred the burden of retirement planning from the government and corporations to the individual.

While some Americans realize that they face a serious retirement funding gap, most are not quite sure what to do about it. A 1994 survey commissioned by Oppenheimer Management Corporation and *Money* magazine found the following:

- Most individuals do not understand the important role that growth-oriented investments like equities should play in retirement planning—nearly half of all preretirees thought bonds frequently outperformed stocks over long periods of time, and 16 percent didn't know which had done better.

- A large number of people do not know how much income they will need to retire comfortably—two-thirds of preretirees believed that they will be able to live comfortably on 60 percent or less of their preretirement income, but only 31 percent of today's retirees said that they were spending 60 percent or less of their preretirement income.

- Most Americans have a severe misperception about the importance of housing as a retirement investment—70 percent of preretirees thought buying a house was one of the best ways for a young person to save for retirement.

Although we're painting a grim picture for these individuals, this shortfall presents tremendous opportunities for financial advisers, as most Americans hoping to retire someday need a lot of help in understanding the basics of investing and developing long-term financial plans now. We believe there are three core issues to focus on:

(1) Individuals need to understand the extent of the retirement gap they are facing. Changes in demographics, increased longevity, and people having children later in life will mean that the financial resources being directed toward retirement will have to last longer and be spread among more people. And Social Security won't be able to rescue them.

(2) People need to take greater advantage of tax-advantaged retirement investments. More than 25 percent of those eligible for 401(k)s do not participate, and many who do participate borrow against their plans. At the same time, contributions to IRAs have dropped by two-thirds since 1986.

(3) Individuals need to understand that over the long term, the stock market has shown slow and steady growth—exactly what's needed to fund a retirement nest egg. People put too much faith in guaranteed investment contracts

(GICs), fixed-income investments, and residential real estate, which in the past have not provided the long-term growth needed to build retirement assets.

HOW MUCH MONEY WILL YOU NEED?

When asked where they expected their retirement income to come from, a group of full-time employees listed the following sources:

Sources of Income during Retirement	Percent of Retirement Income Expected
Employer-sponsored retirement plans	28%
Social Security	26%
Personal investments and savings	16%
IRAs and tax-sheltered annuities	16%
401(k) and thrift plans	14%

As you can see, retirement plans, whether "employer-sponsored," IRAs, tax-sheltered annuities, thrift plans, or 401(k)s, will play a major role in determining your comfort level after you stop working. Whether or not Social Security will continue to exist in its present form twenty or thirty years from now is open to debate. A 1994 survey found that more workers in their twenties and thirties believe in UFOs than in Social Security being around when they retire.

There is always the question of how much money you'll need to fund a comfortable retirement. There is no precise measurement, but it is possible to calculate a rough estimate based upon your income just prior to retirement. (See the chart below for some guidelines.) This is, of course, subject to revision upwards or downwards depending on your needs, your aspirations, your overall financial health, and your changing circumstances.

Annual Income before Retirement	Percent Needed during Retirement	Percent Replaced by Social Security	Percent Needed from Other Sources
$30,000	75%	61%	14%
$50,000	73%	34%	39%
$70,000	74%	24%	50%
$90,000	83%	18%	65%
$150,000	83%	10%	73%
$200,000	85%	5%	80%

BASICS RETIREMENT PLANNING

Let's imagine a hypothetical conversation with the captain of a ship:

> "Captain, how long will it take us to get to our destination?"
> "I don't know."
> "Captain, what are you using for fuel?"
> "I don't know."
> "Captain, do you have a navigation system or crew to help you?"
> "I don't know."
> "Captain, where are we going?"
> "I really don't know."

After hearing these answers, you'd probably want to get off the ship as quickly as possible. However, as bizarre or incredible as this may sound, this is how over 90 percent of us plan our financial future. Most people have no idea how long they'll have to work until they can comfortably retire, what the best investments are for "fueling" their financial future, how to properly gauge the performance of their investments, or what their net worth will be upon retirement.

Careful financial planning is the key to a safe and success-ful "voyage." There are only five steps to every comprehensive financial plan: (1) setting goals, (2) determining specific objectives, (3) developing strategies, (4) setting your plans into motion, and (5) reviewing to check on your progress. To develop an overall plan, however, it's important to both review your current situation—and understand what your goals are. Here's an example of the basic questions a financial planning review would cover:

1. How's your *health*? Are your spouse and dependents healthy?
2. How much *health and disability insurance* do you have? What does it cover? What does it provide?
3. How much *life insurance* do you have?
4. Do you plan to have *children*?
5. How secure is your job? Do you expect your *job status* to change?
6. Do you plan to buy a *home*? What are your monthly *housing* costs?
7. What is your *salary*? Do you expect it to change?
8. What *income tax* bracket are you in?
9. How much money do you think you can put into *savings* annually?
10. How much do you owe in outstanding *debts*?
11. Do you anticipate any *extraordinary financial events*?
12. Do you participate in *retirement plans through work*?
13. What *other investments* do you have (in addition to retirement plans through work)?
14. What are your financial *goals*?
15. What *objectives* will you have to set to reach those goals?
16. What is your *strategy* for reaching those objectives?
17. How will you *implement* that strategy?
18. How often would you like to *review* your progress and your strategies?

Notice that the first three questions deal with insurance. Life, disability, and health insurance are forms of risk transference. You pay someone else (the insurer) a fee so that they will bear a portion or all of the financial consequences due to a physical impairment or death. As unexciting as insurance may be, it is a necessary ingredient of every financial plan. For a large number of people, the only thing between them and successfully reaching their monetary goals is the possibility of an accident or death.

The next three questions cover children, job security, and housing. If you plan to have children, you may need additional life insurance or a larger house. If not, you'll be able to devote more money to your retirement. Job status is also important. If you anticipate changes, or if you are in a high-risk position, you'll have to design your investment plan more conservatively.

Questions seven through nine cover your salary, income taxes, and annual savings. Every investment has tax ramifications, and your tax bracket makes a big difference to your plans—some investments are more appropriate for people in a lower bracket, and some investments are best for those in a high tax bracket. Your ability to save determines how much you can invest each year.

The tenth question, debts, is also very important. Many people have outstanding credit card debts and other loans charging interest rates over 18 percent. It makes no sense whatsoever to be paying an 18 percent credit card rate if your investments earn 5 to 10 percent. Whenever your investments earn less than the rate you are charged for any outstanding debt, you are almost always better off paying off the debt first—even if it means liquidating part of the investment. (Retirement plans usually include a penalty for early withdrawals—these should not be used to pay off debt.)

The question about extraordinary financial events (question 11) covers large expenses that are on the horizon (e.g., paying college tuition, loaning someone some money, buying a boat, etc.), or potential windfalls (e.g., an inheritance or a bonus).

When it comes to company-sponsored retirement plans (question twelve), most people do not fully understand vesting, the value of their retirement account, or the investment options available to them.

Question thirteen covers the value of your existing portfolio and how such moneys are invested. For most people, planning for a 401(k) will involve repositioning part or all of their existing holdings, since the new investment will change their overall investment strategy.

The next two questions cover goals and objectives. *Goals* are things you would like to obtain. Some people have multiple goals; for example (1) to retire comfortably, (2) to buy a house, (3) to send a child through college, (4) to buy a new car every few years, or (5) to take a trip abroad at least once a year. *Objectives* translate goals into dollar figures, meaning that if you want to buy a house, you will need to determine how much the house will cost—your objective in this case being to save enough money to pay for the down payment.

Objectives can be more difficult to analyze. For example, if your goal is a comfortable retirement, you'll have to ask yourself another series of questions: How much income will you need per month? Are you planning to move into less expensive housing? Will the mortgage be paid off? Will your children or other relatives need your financial support?

To determine the size of the nest egg you need to build, you'll need to perform a more complicated analysis based on a number of assumptions: Can you assume that Social Security will be around and that payments will increase at roughly the rate of inflation? What will the rate of inflation be? What rate of return can you expect on your investments—both taxable and tax-sheltered? The other factors are related to the questions answered above: What are your immediate financial needs? How much money can you set aside for retirement? What kind of monthly retirement benefits (or lump-sum payment) can you expect from your employers?

To give you an idea of how this kind of analysis works, let's look at a quick example:

Nan and Joe Lippman, both age 45, have decided to develop a comprehensive plan for their retirement in twenty years (at age 65). Here are the facts established by asking the questions above:

- Both are in excellent health, and both have comprehensive policies through work that include health, medical, major medical, and disability insurance. Neither has life insurance.
- They have no children or plans for children.
- Both have secure jobs. Nan makes $35,000 a year and Joe makes $70,000.
- The couple live in a home that Joe inherited from his parents a few years ago. The house is worth $200,000 and has an existing fixed-rate mortgage that still has twenty years left on it; monthly payments are $1,000.
- The couple is in the 35 percent combined (state and federal) income tax bracket.
- Nan and Joe believe that they can comfortably save $7,000 a year.
- They have no outstanding debts of any kind with the exception of the home mortgage.
- Nan is 100 percent vested in her hospital's retirement

plan. The value of her retirement account is $50,000, invested in a fixed-rate annuity that is renewed each year and currently yields 6 percent. The hospital contributes $3,000 a year on her behalf; Nan does not make any contributions. Joe's company is about to offer a 401(k) plan. For every dollar he contributes, the company will put in fifty cents. The plan is expected to be in place within two months.

- The couple has the following existing assets:

    1. $30,000 in the XYZ Government Bond Fund
    2. $20,000 in Nan's IRA account (100 percent invested in a bank CD that matures in one year)
    3. $15,000 in Joe's IRA account (100 percent invested in the ABC Balanced Mutual Fund)
    4. $10,000 in checking accounts
    5. $100,000 equity in Joe's home

- Their goal is to retire comfortably in twenty years or less.
- Their objective is a monthly retirement income of $4,000, in today's dollars (i.e., adjusted for inflation).
- The couple's overall risk level (the risk they're willing to accept in their investments) is "moderate." They are open to most kinds of investments, but would like to avoid limited partnerships, collectibles (e.g., rare coins, stamps, baseball cards), and "high risk" investments such as futures contracts, most kinds of options, penny stocks, and individual stocks that are not blue chip.
- The couple believes inflation will average 3 percent in the future.

Nan and Joe need to determine what size nest egg will produce the monthly retirement income of $4,000 in *today's dollars* (meaning adjusted for inflation) they want to achieve.

As we have already learned, Nan's retirement account is currently worth $50,000, and yields 6 percent, and the hospital she works for adds $3,000 a year on her behalf. Nan's retirement plan is growing at a real rate of 3 percent per year (6 percent minus 3 percent, the projected rate of inflation). It should be worth $173,010 in twenty years. Let's assume that Joe is going to put $6,000 each year into his new 401(k)— and that his company is going to match 50 percent of his contributions (put in another $3,000). Let's further assume that the combined $9,000 will be invested in a stock portfolio that can be expected to grow 12 percent a year. Joe's retirement account will compound at a 9 percent annual rate (12 percent less the 3 percent inflation rate) for the next twenty years. He should end up with a lump sum of $460,440 in today's dollars.

Joe and Nan's other assets will help them build the nest egg they need: (1) $30,000 in the XYZ Government Bond Fund, (2) $20,000 in Nan's IRA account (invested in a bank CD that matures in one year), (3) $15,000 in Joe's IRA account (invested in the ABC Balanced Mutual Fund), (4) $10,000 in checking accounts, and (5) $100,000 equity in Joe's home. The couple has told you that they do not plan on changing homes, so any increase in this value will not have a direct impact on their retirement. Let us also assume that Nan and Joe want to keep the $10,000 in their checking account for emergency purposes and to pay monthly bills. This means that the remaining $65,000 of their assets can be repositioned into investments that earn better returns. These investments, after adjustments for tax status and inflation, can be expected to grow to the impressive total figure of $327,400 after twenty years.

Earlier, we learned that the couple can comfortably save $7,000 a year. This figure must now be reduced by $6,000, the amount Joe will be contributing to his new 401(k) plan. This means that the couple still has $1,000 to invest each year. Assuming a 12 percent rate of growth, adjusted to 9 percent after deducting for inflation, $1,000 each year will grow to $51,160 in twenty years.

Here are the total dollar figures:

$173,010	Nan's retirement plan
$460,440	Joe's retirement plan
$327,400	Other investments
$51,160	Annual savings
$1,012,010	Total

In twenty years the couple will end up with over a million dollars, adjusted for inflation. Investing that $1,000,000 (let's use round numbers to make the final measurements easy) at 8 percent will produce $80,000 a year in earned interest, or $6,667 per month—a figure much higher than their goal of $4,000 per month. By the way, the $6,667 monthly figure does not include Social Security benefits, which could be $700 to $1,200 *per person* each month.

Nan and Joe are, obviously, fortunate. They should have no difficulty in reaching their goals. Their *strategy* was to find investments that fit their risk level and still met their financial objectives.

As you can see, developing a strategy for your 401(k) investments is influenced by your overall financial situation. Note especially the importance of Joe's contribution to his new 401(k) plan to the couple's overall financial success.

In order to make the right choices for your 401(k), you'll have to make similar calculations based on your own answers to the questions asked at the beginning of the chapter. Your calculations, like those in the example, will depend on a few assumptions and calculations about the future performance of your investment choices. For most people, repositioning part or all of their existing holdings is very likely once a plan is developed. If you need help reviewing your holdings, contact the Institute of Certified Fund Specialists (800-848-2029) for a list of certified advisers in your area.

The core issue at the heart of retirement planning is how to choose the investment options that fit your needs and investment style. 401(k)s offer the entire range of investment possibilities. How can you be sure that you've chosen the one that will make the most of your resources, and allow you to enjoy a comfortable retirement? The chapter that follows will introduce you to the basic—and best—investment strategies to follow in your 401(k) plan.

CHAPTER 6
401(k) Investment Strategies

You have a basic decision to make: Will your future standard of living be maintained, enhanced—or left to the whims of fate or politicians? When it comes to basic "quality of life" issues—what you will be able to afford to buy in the future, or where you will live—will be decided by what you do today.

You may think that *your* money is safe. You may have it invested in bank CDs, in a passbook savings account, or in T-bills (U.S. Treasuries). What most people fail to take into account is the *double* "taxation" their money is subjected to: inflation and income taxes. (Eventually, even your 401(k) plan will be taxed—when you make withdrawals from it.)

Look at the table that follows. See how one of the most popular "safe" investments, U.S. Treasury bills, has really fared over the past twenty-five years. The far right column, "Real Rate of T-Bill Return," shows how U.S. Treasury bills have performed on an after-tax, after-inflation basis. The real rate of return is also very similar to what the most popular investment, bank CDs, has returned. (CD rates are usually a little higher than those offered by T-bills, but not always.)

Real Rates of Return

Year	T-Bill Rate	Federal Tax Rate	After-Tax Return	Inflation Rate	Real Rate of T-Bill Return
1970	6.48%	50%	3.24%	5.6%	-2.23%
1971	4.51%	50%	2.26%	3.3%	-1.01%
1972	4.48%	50%	2.24%	3.4%	-1.12%
1973	7.20%	50%	3.60%	8.7%	-4.69%
1974	7.94%	62%	3.02%	12.3%	-8.27%
1975	6.09%	62%	2.31%	6.9%	-4.29%
1976	5.25%	62%	2.00%	4.9%	-2.77%
1977	5.53%	60%	2.21%	6.7%	-4.21%
1978	7.58%	60%	3.03%	9.0%	-5.48%
1979	10.06%	59%	4.12%	13.3%	-8.10%
1980	11.37%	59%	4.66%	12.5%	-6.97%
1981	13.80%	59%	5.66%	8.9%	-2.98%
1982	11.07%	50%	5.54%	3.8%	1.67%
1983	8.73%	48%	4.54%	3.8%	0.71%
1984	9.76%	45%	5.37%	3.9%	1.41%
1985	7.65%	45%	4.21%	3.8%	0.39%
1986	6.03%	45%	3.32%	1.1%	2.19%
1987	6.03%	38%	3.74%	4.4%	-0.63%
1988	6.91%	33%	4.63%	4.4%	0.22%
1989	8.03%	33%	5.38%	4.6%	0.75%
1990	7.46%	31%	5.15%	6.1%	-0.90%
1991	5.44%	31%	3.75%	3.1%	0.63%
1992	3.51%	31%	2.42%	2.9%	-0.46%
1993	2.90%	31%	2.00%	2.8%	-0.78%
1994	3.90%	31%	2.69%	2.7%	-0.01%
1995	5.51%	31%	3.80%	2.7%	1.10%

How would you feel about someone who recommended an investment to you that had lost money, after adjustments for inflation and taxes, two-thirds of the time (seventeen of the last twenty-six years)? What do all of these depressing figures mean? The answer is surprisingly obvious: Every investment is subject to one or more types of risk. There is no way around this "law of nature." Investments that offer a guaranteed rate of return (e.g., bank CDs, government securities, etc.) would be fine if we lived in a country that had fixed costs. However, this is not likely to happen during your investment lifetime. You will always be at risk from the effects of inflation on your "nest egg."

FISH OR CUT BAIT

Unfortunately, there is never an ideal time to invest. Stock prices never fall or rise as fast as we expect, and our predictions for interest rates never quite come true. Trying to predict the best time to invest will leave you in a familiar position: "Gee. I wish I had bought _____ when it was at _____ ." (You fill in the blanks.)

The time to invest is now. If you don't like stocks, invest in bonds, real estate investment trusts (REITs), or foreign securities. Better yet, include stocks by investing in them a little at a time, say $100 to $700 a month. By investing a set amount each month, you can make this volatility work on your behalf. If you don't like bonds because you are certain that interest rates are headed upward, then invest in a money market fund—something that benefits from rising rates. Similarly, if you think real estate prices are too low, start adding money over the next few years into a real estate investment trust.

It is always easy to make the case against investing at a given point in time. And it's just as easy to be dead wrong. Just before Operation Desert Storm almost every major brokerage firm told its clients to get out of stocks. Yet, during this three-week period, stocks posted a gain of over 15 percent. (Just think what that would equal if you could *annualize* such a short-term upswing—a 260+ percent rate of return!) There was an even more compelling reason not to invest in the stock market in 1991: the recession. Funny, but the stock market did not seem to mind the recession that year. It posted one of its biggest gains, up over 30 percent in one year. (Actually, stocks have gone up during seven of the last eight recessions.)

Or look back to early 1981. There were plenty of reasons not to invest in bonds. The prime interest rate had passed 20 percent and was expected to hit 25 to 30 percent within a year (it peaked at 21.5 percent). Within a few months, the bond market reversed itself, and these debt instruments went on to post their best decade ever. Finally, look at real estate. Until the mid-1960s, *residential* real estate was considered a poor investment. We all know what happened to home prices in many parts of the country during the next twenty years.

Is there a lesson to be learned from all of these wonderful stories? In reality, investments that are out of favor—as long as they are fundamentally sound—are "on sale." Prices rise and fall in every type of investment, and the right time to buy is when the investment is underpriced—not when prices are at their highest. Buy when there are opportunities! As Sir John Templeton, the grandfather of international investing, the founder of the Templeton Mutual Funds, and the person who is heralded as having the best long-term track record when it comes to investing, once said, "The best place to invest is where pessimism is the highest." (e.g., Hong Kong right after Tiananmen Square, the United States during its 1991 recession, etc.)

Fortunately, there are investments that will benefit from virtually any economic circumstance. For example, during the Great Depression in the late 1920s and early 1930s, long-term U.S. government bonds appreciated almost 200 percent (not bad when you consider that U.S. Treasury bills yielded less than 1 percent). During the inflationary years of the late 1970s and early 1980s, when long-term bonds took a beating, common stocks and mutual funds that invested in stocks soared in value. And while Wall Street concentrated on stocks and bonds during the mid and late 1980s, real estate prices in many parts of the country rose handsomely. For the first half of the 1990s, we have seen the emerging markets soar and then nose-dive, while the U.S. dollar weakened and its securities strengthened. The 1994 calendar year marked the worst year for domestic bonds in over half a century, yet U.S. stocks still managed to post a slight gain.

No matter how bad economic conditions look, no matter what the newspapers, magazines, and television commentators tell you, there are always opportunities available to the savvy investor. When stocks and/or bonds seem to be going nowhere in this country, they are probably appreciating briskly in Hong Kong, Sweden, Japan, the United Kingdom, France, or Taiwan. The trick, of course, is to determine what the *next* "hot spot" will be. Since no one really knows what stocks, bonds, or real estate will do next week, much less next year or over the course of a decade, we need to come up with a game plan or course of action that factors in these investment realities.

Do not think for a minute that you are going to get rich quick. Instead, you can learn to get rich *slowly*. This may not sound very exciting, and perhaps it is not the stuff that best-sellers are made of, but it is the focus of this book.

INVEST EARLY, INVEST OFTEN

As with all retirement plans, the key to putting aside the money you need is starting as early as possible. The timing of your decision to begin saving for your retirement is critical. While you may still have quite a few years until you retire, it is important that you start to save for your retirement as early as possible. As you can see from the illustration below, the more time you give your investments to grow, the better. It compares three different 401(k) investors, each earning a 10 percent return, but each investing at different stages in their working career.

The "Early Investor" started investing in 1995 and contributed $9,240 (the maximum limit for the 1995 calendar year) to a 401(k) every year for ten years. The "Late Investor" started in 2004 (ten years later than the Early Investor) and also contributed $9,240, but for eleven years, through 2014. The "Smart Investor" started in 1995 and contributed $9,240 every year for twenty years.

Year	Early Investor	Late Investor	Smart Investor
1995	$9,240	—	$9,240
1996	$9,240	—	$9,240
1997	$9,240	—	$9,240
1998	$9,240	—	$9,240
1999	$9,240	—	$9,240
2000	$9,240	—	$9,240
2001	$9,240	—	$9,240
2002	$9,240	—	$9,240
2003	$9,240	—	$9,240
2004	$9,240	$9,240	$9,240
2005	—	$9,240	$9,240
2006	—	$9,240	$9,240
2007	—	$9,240	$9,240
2008	—	$9,240	$9,240
2009	—	$9,240	$9,240
2010	—	$9,240	$9,240
2011	—	$9,240	$9,240
2012	—	$9,240	$9,240

2013	—	$9,240	$9,240
2014	—	$9,240	$9,240
Total invested	$92,400	$101,640	$184,800
Total account value at the end of 2014	$381,470	$171,220	$529,270

As you can see, the Early Investor, who contributed a total of $92,400 over ten years, saw his investment multiply by a factor of over four. The Late Investor, who contributed a total of $101,640, saw his investment not even double. The Smart Investor saw her investment grow by a factor of well over two. Thus, even though the Smart Investor ended up with the most money, it is the Early Investor who enjoyed the greatest compounding effect.

The example above points out the benefits of investing as soon as possible and as frequently as possible. As a point of interest, you may be interested in knowing that even if the Late Investor contributed an additional $9,240 for thirty more years (for a total of forty-one contributions of $9,240 each), he would still not end up with as much as the Early Investor, who contributed $9,240 for only ten years. The Early Investor ends up with $6,656,650 in thirty more years, and the Late Investor has an ending balance of $4,507,730 if thirty more years are tacked on. This is further proof of the power of compounding and making investments sooner rather than later.

MAXIMIZING THE TAX ADVANTAGE OF YOUR 401(K)

There are two major tax advantages to contributing to a 401(k):

1. You receive a deduction for the contribution, and
2. The investment's growth in value is not subject to current taxation. This is known as "sheltered growth."

To give you an idea of the benefits of tax-deferred growth, let's look at an example that compares two different investments.

Suppose you have two investments, X and Y, both of which are expected to grow at 12 percent a year and involve similar risks. Investment X is not tax-advantaged or sheltered in any way; you can expect the entire 12 percent in growth to be taxed each year. Investment Y is similar enough that it would be subject to the same taxes, but since it is part of a 401(k), the taxes will not come into play until money is withdrawn. Further suppose that you have $9,000 to invest, are in a 33 percent combined federal and state income tax bracket, and at age 41, expect to retire in twenty-four years, at age 65.

An investment growing at 12 percent pretax and 8 percent after tax will double in value every nine years. This means that investment X will double in value from $9,000 to $18,000 at the end of the first nine years and then double again to $36,000 at the end of the second nine years. Over the remaining six years (nine plus nine plus six equals twenty-four years), $36,000 will grow to $57,060.

Investment Y, growing at the same 12 percent pretax rate, grows faster, since it is not penalized by taxes each year. At a 12 percent rate of growth, money doubles every six years. This means that the original $9,000 will grow to $18,000 in six years, $36,000 in twelve years, $72,000 in eighteen years, and $144,000 in twenty-four years.

There is a catch. Investment Y ($57,0600 certainly looks more appealing than investment X ($144,000), but investment Y has *not yet been taxed*.

A common mistake most financial advisers make is evaluating investment Y ($144,000) after income taxes have been subtracted. In the majority of cases, however, this is an unrealistic approach. On retirement, most people are going to be looking for current *income*, rather than long-term growth. Since investment Y can be rolled over, along with the rest of your 401(k), into an IRA, income taxes can be further deferred. Moreover, you can switch the entire $144,000 into a series of income-oriented investments.

A $144,000 investment earning 8 percent—and still sheltered within a 401(k) or IRA—will throw off $11,520 a year. (If withdrawn, this would be taxable income.) Investment X, also earning 8 percent a year, will generate only $4,565 a year. The difference between these two figures is "only" $6,955, or 152 percent more for every year of your retirement.

The percentage of difference, 152 percent in this example, is extreme enough so that, hopefully, you will add more money to your 401(k) each year, rather than making the one-time investment used in this example. If we repeat the comparison between X and Y, but invest $9,000 *each year*, the results become much more dramatic: X grows to $600,930 and Y grows to $1,063,440. And as before, by rolling the money over into an 8 percent taxable investment, would you rather receive $48,074 (investment X) or $85,075 each year (investment Y)?

As you can see from this example, the sheltering advantages of participating in a 401(k) can be tremendously beneficial. Your money will grow and compound faster; the longer the period of time and the greater the number of contributions, the greater impact compounding will have. We won't go through the math, but the tax advantages become even more dramatic if you are in a higher combined tax bracket, such as 35 to 41 percent. However, even if you are in a 15 percent federal bracket and a 5 percent state bracket, the difference between using sheltered and unsheltered growth is significant.

Another advantage of 401(k) investing is that the contributions are made pretax—deducted from your salary before your taxes are calculated. Pretax contributions means that you can afford to invest more money in your 401(k) plan.

For example, assume that John has a salary of $45,000 a year and is able to contribute $3,000 to his 401(k) plan for the year (the maximum per calendar year is over $9,000). Instead of his W-2 showing $45,000 in income, it will now show $42,000. Assuming a 28 percent federal income tax bracket, John's tax bill for the year has been lowered by $840 (28 percent x $3,000). In essence, John has paid $2,160 for his $3,000 investment—already a good return. If John continues to make $3,000 contributions for a total of twenty years, and the 401(k) account averages 10 percent in growth per year, it will grow to $189,000 at the end of twenty years.

If, in the example above, John were to liquidate his $189,000 retirement account, he would net $136,100 after paying taxes (this assumes paying 28 percent federal taxes on the entire $189,000).

If, instead, John had *not* set up a 401(k), but had invested his $3,000 in a regular investment account, the results would be very different. First, he would have used after-tax dollars instead of before-tax dollars to fund the investment. Out of the same $3,000 in pretax income, John's annual investment would have dropped to $2,160, after the 28 percent tax. Second, the money would not grow and compound tax-deferred. Instead of growing at 10 percent, the money would grow at 7.2 percent (10 percent minus federal taxes of 28 percent). At the end of twenty years, this nonqualified retirement account would be worth only $97,200 after paying all federal taxes.

The difference in the example above becomes even more dramatic if (1) you factor in state income taxes, (2) you make contributions for more than twenty years, (3) you assume a higher growth rate, or, most important, (4) you make a larger dollar investment each year or (5) your employer makes a matching contribution (even a token one) each year.

WHERE SHOULD YOUR MONEY BE?

One of the most difficult decisions you will have to make is deciding how your 401(k) contributions should be invested. Every investment that has ever existed, that exists today, or that will come into being in the future falls into one of three general categories: equity, debt, or hybrid. For the most part, equities are more volatile than debt instruments; hybrids fall somewhere in between on the risk spectrum.

When you invest in an *equity instrument*, you become an owner. Either you own the asset outright or you become a co-owner. For example, when you buy even one share of IBM or GM stock, you become one of the company's owners. True, these companies have tens or hundreds of thousands of "owners" (stockholders), but with a small investment, you have now entered the ranks of corporate America. Equity investments include (1) domestic and foreign common stocks, (2) preferred stocks, (3) equity in a home, (4) partial or complete ownership of a business, (5) commodities, and (6) a mutual fund, limited partnership, or other entity that invests in any of these things (e.g., a limited partnership that buys oil and gas fields, a real estate investment trust, a mutual fund that invests in U.S. and foreign stocks, a variable annuity subaccount that invests in growth and income stocks). A *commodity* is anything that comes from the ground (e.g., gold, silver, and other metals), grows on the ground (e.g., corn, wheat, oranges, soybeans, coffee), or feeds from the ground (e.g., cattle, pigs, chickens).

When you invest in a *debt instrument*, you are lending your money to someone else or to some entity, such as a bank, government, or corporation. In return for the use of your money, your debtor agrees to pay you a fee, known more commonly as *interest*. As long as the debtor uses your money, the debtor is expected to pay you interest. When they are through using your money, they are expected to pay it back. Once your principal has been returned, the interest payments stop. The most common examples of debt instruments are (1) any investment (or security) issued by the U.S. government or one of its agencies (e.g., Treasury bills, Treasury notes, Treasury bonds, EE bonds, GNMAs, FNMAs), (2) securities issued by a state or one of its municipalities (e.g., tax-free bonds and notes), (3) certificates of deposit (CDs), (4) money market accounts and interest-bearing checking accounts, (5) corporate bonds and notes (sometimes referred to as "commercial paper"), (6) a mutual fund, limited partnership, or other entity that invests in any of these things (e.g., a limited partnership that buys mortgage-backed securities, a mutual fund that invests in government bonds, a variable annuity subaccount that invests in corporate bonds), and (7) fixed-rate annuities.

There are a handful of investments that are *hybrid* in nature, part equity and part debt. This means that in some respects they act or perform like equities, while in others they are like debt instruments. Hybrid instruments include (1) balanced mutual funds and variable annuity subaccounts, (2) convertible securities mutual funds and variable annuity subaccounts, and (3) high-yield bond funds and variable annuity subaccounts.

Most 401(k) plans do not offer all of the categories described above. However, the great majority offer employees variations on several of these categories. A quick review of these variations or "name changes" may be helpful to you. We will begin with common stocks.

Chances are your 401(k) plan offers a growth fund or

growth portfolio. Such an investment is made up of stocks. If your 401(k) plan has a bond portfolio, it is most likely a long-term government bond fund or a long-term corporate bond fund. In this case, the maturity of the bonds in the account (when the bonds come due) is much more important than whether they were issued by the government or a high-quality corporation. Even though bonds are a very popular investment, you will probably be given only one bond fund or portfolio to choose from.

Technically, high-yield bonds are debt instruments since you do not own part of a company (unlike with a stock, which represents an ownership interest). However, a number of financial publications consider high-yield bonds to be a hybrid because somewhere between 30 and 70 percent of their movement is attributable to economic news (whereas 100 percent of a government bond's price movement is based on interest rates or investors "fleeing to quality" during negative or uncertain political or economic events). Balanced funds and subaccounts invest part of their portfolio in stocks and the balance in bonds; these types of portfolios may also invest in money market instruments (e.g., commercial paper, U.S. Treasury bills, and bank CDs) and preferred stocks and convertibles. A convertible security is an instrument that can be converted into the common stock of the issuing corporation.

Your 401(k) plan may also allow you to invest in your company's stock (an equity) or to purchase life insurance with before-tax dollars (paying life insurance premiums and getting a tax deduction). How the cash value of the life insurance is invested will determine whether you are participating in an equity, debt, or a hybrid investment. If the cash value of each premium payment is invested in a variable product and you determine that the money is to be invested in a stock portfolio, then the life insurance is an equity instrument. If the cash value is invested so that you have a guaranteed rate of return or if it is invested in a variable product that invests in bonds or money market instruments, the life insurance is a debt instrument.

Finally, it is a virtual certainty that your 401(k) will include a money market account or *CD* (certificate of deposit). If your plan is overseen by an insurance company, the counterpart of these "cash-type" investments would be a fixed-rate annuity or GIC (guaranteed investment contract). Fixed-rate annuities and GICs act just like bank CDs: You lock in a specific rate that is guaranteed for the lock-in period, which can range from several weeks to several years. All of these investments are similar in risk and performance to U.S. Treasury bills.

Since no one is going to watch over your money as care-fully as you will, it is critical that you have a basic under-standing of what you can expect from your investments, both inside and outside of your 401(k). If you understand how well or how poorly an investment can fare, you will feel more com-fortable with whatever choices you make. Generally, people are the most afraid of things they do not understand. Investment books and brokers will readily tell you how well something will perform, but they rarely mention how ugly the same investment can become during certain periods.

Not all investments are appropriate for your 401(k). For example, the *only* way to make the interest on municipal bonds or tax-free money market funds taxable is to put them inside a qualified retirement plan. These investments would still grow tax-deferred, but the interest earned would be fully taxable when the 401(k) was liquidated. The same is true of Series EE bonds. Residential and income-producing real estate cannot be part of your 401(k), since the IRS classifies such things as being either "self-dealing" or "constructive receipt" (meaning that you are buying or selling something you either control or could have use or enjoyment from).

Should your 401(k) be invested primarily in equities, debt instruments, or both? The answer is, *It depends*. It depends upon how long you plan on investing, how much risk or volatility you can stand, the makeup of your existing portfolio, and any biases you may have for or against specific investments.

HOLDING PERIOD

How long you plan to hold on to an investment is a critical aspect of your investment planning. The longer your time frame, the more predictable and attractive equities—or stocks—become. If your investment horizon is less than three years, most, if not all, of your assets should be in debt instruments. If you can hold on to an investment for three to seven years, these funds should be evenly divided between equity and debt instruments. Finally, if your time horizon is over eight years, then the bulk of your holdings should be in equities.

Much advice on how to determine a holding period can be confusing when it comes to retirement accounts such as IRAs, Keoghs, and 401(k) plans. Your time horizon should be based on your life expectancy, *not* on when you plan to retire. After all, expenses do not cease once you retire, and you do not get some special compensation for the continued effects of inflation or income taxes. What all this means is that your tolerance for equity-oriented investments should be extended.

The timing for phasing in your investments from lump sums (rollover accounts from a previous retirement plan) varies quite a bit depending upon one's age and risk level. In general, the closer you are to retirement, the more extended the period should be. The same is true for risk level: The more conservative you are, the longer the phase-in period. The number of months suggested for phasing in any lump sum are somewhat arbitrary. However, it is very doubtful that even the most conservative investor would stretch out a bond invest-ment for more than a year (since bonds rarely have two nega-tive years back to back) or a stock investment for more than eighteen months (since the worst period we have experienced in the stock market over the past fifty years was the 1973–74 recession when stocks lost value for seventeen months).

RISK

One of the best ways to look at any 401(k) investment is what is known as the "apple juice analogy." Imagine that you have a pitcher that contains exactly eight ounces of apple juice. Next to that pitcher are two glasses. Each glass also holds up to eight ounces. One glass is labeled "safety;" the other, "potential return." You can pour the eight ounces into one or both glasses; the more you pour into one glass, the less you'll have left for the other. Likewise, every investment you can think of has "eight ounces" of benefits. No matter how wild or how boring you think something is, it still has exactly eight ounces, no more and no less. The greater the risk (the less "safety"), the greater the reward. Here are a couple of exam-ples of how this apple juice analogy works:

Let's say you that are thinking about buying long-term U.S. government bonds. As you will learn in a later chapter, government bonds are very safe (five or six ounces in the "safety" glass), but have only fair potential for appreciation (one or two ounces in the "return" glass). Common stocks, on the other hand, range from poor to good (zero to two ounces) in terms of safety, but have very good, and sometimes excel-lent, potential for total return (six to eight ounces). As you can see, both common stocks and government bonds offer investors exactly eight ounces of benefits.

All investment guidelines come with one big caveat: they should reflect the level of risk you are comfortable with. Thus, a very conservative investor with an investment holding period of, say, ten years, is probably better off, in the interest of not losing too much sleep, with a portfolio weighted towards debt vehicles. Conversely, an aggressive investor planning to retire in a year or two may want to "go for the gusto" and put everything into common stocks.

It's important to remember that there are risks besides outright losses in value. One of the most important is purchasing-power risk (the effects of inflation). Some investments that are traditionally thought of as conservative, such as government securities, money market funds, and bank CDs, actually have quite a bit of purchasing-power risk. As an example, if you buy a twenty-year government bond for $1,000, the bond is guaranteed to be worth $1,000 in twenty years—but does anyone doubt that $1,000 will buy much less in twenty years than it does today?

There is also the risk of taxation. Fortunately, money in 401(k) and other qualified retirement accounts, as well as annuities, grows and compounds tax-deferred (not tax-free). This does not mean that you do not have to think about taxes. If you have investments outside of your qualified retirement accounts, then taxation is an issue with that portion of your portfolio.

No matter how conservative you believe you are when it comes to investment risk, consider the following fact: Over the past half century, the very *best* twenty years in a row for bonds is barely better (by less than 1 percent per year) than the very *worst* twenty years in a row for stocks. This means that if you are ultraconservative and under age 65 (which means you have a remaining life expectancy of about twenty years or more), you should probably have *at least* a moderate

(20 to 35 percent) exposure to stocks.

A *properly* diversified portfolio can reduce your risk level without decreasing return. A properly diversified portfolio is one that includes different types of investment categories (e.g., growth funds, high-yield bonds, etc.) that do not all move up and down together at the same time. This means that when the growth stocks in your portfolio are going down, the high-yield bond portion (or some other category) may be either maintaining its value or actually going up in value.

Most 401(k) plans make it possible to diversify within the plan. Otherwise, you should look to your entire investment portfolio for opportunities to diversify.

In order to help you identify your own tolerance for risk, here are descriptions of six categories of investors, ranked by their risk-tolerance. (This will come in handy in the chapter that follows, as well.)

Aggressive investor—Someone who limits his or her portfolio to only stocks (with perhaps a little exposure to options—just for some fun and excitement). The aggressive investor is not satisfied with averaging 10 to 15 percent a year; he or she wants the chance to average 16 to 18 percent or more annually. The aggressive investor will regularly see at least part of the portfolio go up or down 20 to 30 percent. Such high returns (and losses) can be obtained only by concentrating on a few individual stocks or sector funds (a portfolio that invests in one country other than the United States or a single industry group, such as computer or auto stocks).

Fairly aggressive investor—A person or couple who will always be 100 percent in stocks or funds that invest in stocks, but not always of the most volatile type.

Moderate investor—An investor who realizes that in order to average 10 percent or more per year, a certain amount of volatility has to be accepted. The moderate investor understands that once in a while he or she will suffer a 10 to 15 percent loss for the year. However, this same investor also knows that such a loss can be followed by a 20 to 30 percent gain the following year. The moderate investor will always have a majority of his or her holdings in stocks or professionally managed portfolios (e.g., mutual funds, variable annuity subaccounts, etc.) that invest in stocks. It is not unrealistic for the moderate investor to have a portfolio in which equities represent 75 to 100 percent of the total.

Moderate-to-conservative investor—An individual or couple that feels fairly comfortable with the ups and downs of the stock market, as long as equities make up no more than 65 percent of their portfolio.

Conservative investor—Someone who can accept an overall portfolio loss of somewhere between 0 and 5 percent (approximately). This kind of investor does not want to take any big risks, even with a small part of the portfolio; however, he or she does not want to have all of his or her holdings in things such as money market accounts and short-term bonds. The conservative investor realizes that inflation is harmful, but does not worry a lot about it. No matter how good things look, the conservative investor will probably never have more than a third of the total portfolio committed to stocks.

Ultraconservative investor—A person who is unwilling to have (or cannot accept) an overall portfolio loss for any given year. This person is willing to have a moderate loss (up to 5 percent) in one or a couple of different investments, but only if such losses are offset by gains, interest, or dividends in other parts of the portfolio. The ultraconservative investor is much more concerned with account statement losses than with what inflation might do to his or her standard of living now or in the future. Stocks will never represent more than a fourth of the total portfolio.

CURRENT HOLDINGS

Before you make any investments in your 401(k), you should review your current holdings. Your goal should be to not have too large a part of your entire portfolio invested in any one kind of investment—and any naturally tax-advantaged investments *outside* your 401(k).

The prudent course of action, of course, is to construct a portfolio that includes a range of different asset categories (e.g., real estate, U.S. securities, foreign securities, etc.). If you have $50,000 invested in common stocks, plus a 401(k) worth $10,000, your portfolio diversification strategy should be based on the entire $60,000, not just the $10,000 or $50,000 account.

A diversified portfolio will not only protect you against the ups and downs of any given asset class (since not all of your investments are likely to suffer equally at once), but will protect you from your own biases, and the biases of your information sources (e.g., a stockbroker who loves IBM, that pundit who guarantees that he knows when to get out of the market, or the person on television who shows how easy it is to make a million buying distressed properties).

Whatever your risk level, try to reposition any moderate- or high-interest-bearing securities (or high-dividend-paying stocks or mutual funds) so that they are within your 401(k) or other sheltered accounts. If your retirement accounts are not large enough to take in the entire amount (e.g., if you have

$30,000 in a high-yield bond fund that is not part of a retirement account and you also have 401(k) and IRA accounts whose combined total value is $19,000), shift as much as you can (which would be $19,000 in this example). Shifting, in this case, refers to selling the high-yield fund owned outside the 401(k); replacing it, also outside the 401(k), with a tax-deferred or growth oriented investment; selling the investments inside the 401(k), and replacing them, inside the plan, with a high-yield bond fund. The sole purpose of this kind of repositioning is to reduce your current income taxes. Do not be overly concerned that you might have to sell the XYZ High-Yield Bond Fund and replace it with the ABC High-Yield Bond Fund. There are a large number of good (or great) mutual funds and variable annuities in every investment category.

Finally, a portfolio needs to take into account any biases you may have. For better or worse, each of us has different experiences, perspectives and beliefs. Whatever their origin, these biases need to be kept under control if you want to build a successful retirement portfolio.

For example, if you inherited 5,000 shares of a utility company stock with the understanding that you would never sell it, your other investment decisions should "work around" or complement this core holding. You should probably not consider new investments in utility stocks for the balance of your portfolio. Similarly, even though common stocks are an excellent addition to most portfolios, you may, for one reason or another, refuse to own them. This means that other parts of your portfolio will need to be designed to compensate for this "shortcoming."

DON'T TRY TO PREDICT THE FUTURE

Look at the table that follows (labeled "26 Years of Annual Total Returns"). Notice that none of the four categories does

well each and every year. Notice also that it would be impossible to predict a trend or pattern.

If you could be certain about the future rate of return on
each asset class, the process of picking the perfect category
for your 401(k) would be easy: Invest all of your capital in
the asset with the highest forecasted return. However, since
future returns are uncertain and since returns on some asset
classes are more uncertain than those on others, you *must*
diversify.

26 Years of Annual Total Returns (1970–1995)

Year	U.S. Stocks	U.S. Bonds	Foreign Stocks	Foreign Bonds
1970	+4%	+18%	-10%	+9%
1971	+14%	+11%	+31%	+23%
1972	+19%	+7%	+37%	+5%
1973	-15%	+2%	-14%	+6%
1974	-26%	-6%	-22%	+5%
1975	+37%	+17%	+37%	+9%
1976	+24%	+19%	+4%	+11%
1977	-7%	+3%	+19%	+39%
1978	+6%	+0%	+34%	+18%
1979	+19%	-2%	+6%	-5%
1980	+32%	+0%	+24%	+14%
1981	-5%	+3%	-1%	-5%
1982	+22%	+39%	-1%	+12%
1983	+23%	+9%	+25%	+4%
1984	+6%	+17%	+8%	-2%
1985	+32%	+24%	+57%	+37%
1986	+19%	+16%	+70%	+34%
1987	+5%	+0%	+25%	+36%
1988	+17%	+8%	+27%	+3%
1989	+32%	+7%	+11%	+10%

1990	-1%	+6%	-23%	+15%
1991	+31%	+16%	+13%	+3%
1992	+8%	+8%	-12%	+5%
1993	+10%	+18%	+33%	+15%
1994	+1%	-8%	+8%	+7%
1995	+34%	+30%	+8%	+15%
Number of times "best"	7	5	9	5

Babe Ruth hit more home runs than just about anyone else, but he also struck out more than most baseball players. As an investor, your goal should be, by analogy, to hit doubles and triples. You'll have to accept that you'll never hit a "home run" (since not all of your money will be tied up in just one asset), but you will sleep better at night knowing that you will not "strike-out." Such a strategy translates into returns that are better than what 98 percent of all other investors are doing. The 1 or 2 percent who end up doing better than you will have taken substantially greater risks.

The next chapter is rather long, but you will need to read only a few pages of it. After you have read the introductory pages, you can go directly to the "case study" closest to your own situation and see how your 401(k) account should be structured. Expected rates of return are also provided.

After you have finished reading the next few chapters, which take a closer look at specific investment classes, your thinking about investing will change. Perhaps for the first time you will clearly understand how these things called "investments" work—their strengths and weaknesses. Don't think that you need financial experience or an MBA to understand these investment choices—you do not. This book was written for people who want to learn.

CHAPTER 7
Case Studies

This chapter shows you where your money should be invested based on your age and your tolerance for risk. The model portfolios presented are based on specific age ranges and situations (e.g., single, married, children about to go to college, etc.). Five different combinations of age and marital status are represented:

1	2	3	4	5
Age 40 or less	Age 50 or less	Age 41 to 60	Age 51 to 60	Over 61
Single	Married	Single	Married	Single or married

Within each of these five different age and marital status combinations, six different portfolio positions are given, depending upon the individual or couple's risk level.

A = ultraconservative   C = conservative to moderate   E = fairly aggressive
B = conservative   D = moderate   F = aggressive

As a result, a total of thirty portfolios are described below. By combining the two tables above, you can quickly go to the case study that best describes you. As an example, if you are married and between the ages of 51 and 60 (the case studies that begin with a 4), and you are a conservative investor (the case studies that end with a B), you should go directly to case study 4B.

If you are not quite sure what risk level you are, start with the more conservative of the two levels you are considering. After a year or two, you can always shift into a more aggressive (or stock-oriented) portfolio. For the longer haul (five years or more), if you are going to err, it is actually better to be a little more aggressive. First, chances are (hopefully) that the emergencies you think you need cash for will never happen. Second, the cumulative effects of inflation are probably much greater than you think. Finally, and most importantly, your life does not end at age 65. The fact that your stocks or bonds are down on your 64th or 65th birthday does not mean that they will not have a tremendous comeback when you reach age 66, 67, or 68. Your investment portfolio is a lifelong idea, not one that ends at your retirement.

The case studies show net returns (after deducting any buying and selling costs or management fees). For any given year or two, the results you experience may be higher or lower than what is shown, particularly if your tolerance for risk is moderate or higher. However, the numbers become much more accurate if you look at returns over a period of five years or more.

In a number of cases, there are minor changes from one age group (or marital status) to another at a particular risk level. The reason for this is that the parameters given are rather narrow, and it is assumed that your investment options are somewhat limited (e.g., you do not have access to a global bond, real estate, or gold fund). Finally, you will notice that in some cases very similar or identical results are expected from one case study to another, even though there have been some changes in the investment categories and weightings. There is more than one way to get a 9 percent or 13 percent projected return.

One final note. These case studies are recommendations

only. In every case, you should consider your personal financial resources and style before making a decision that fits your retirement needs.

Case Study 1A: *Age 40 or less, single, and an ultraconservative investor.*

Money to be invested: Periodic contributions for the next fifteen to twenty-five years (see comments below if there is also a lump sum to be invested).

Although the ultraconservative investor should have at least half of the portfolio in equities (due to age), he or she will not make such a commitment. The ultraconservative investor does not fully understand stocks and is always fearful that there will be a market crash or correction.

Recommended Investments and Weightings for Each Category

30 percent	intermediate-term government bonds (bonds that mature in six to ten years)
30 percent	long-term government or corporate bond fund (maturity of over ten years)
10 percent	balanced funds (funds that invest in both stocks and bonds)
10 percent	global equities (U.S. and foreign stocks from the major economies)
10 percent	high-yield bonds (bonds with interest payments that are about 2 percent higher than those on government bonds)
10 percent	utilities (sometimes considered boring, but usually stable and predictable)

This portfolio has 75 percent of its assets in bonds and 25 percent in stocks. The overall return for this diversified portfolio should be in the 8 to 9 percent range.

If there is a lump sum to be invested (a retirement account being transferred in from a former employer), the same mix can be used, but only half of the lump sum should be invested immediately, the other half (which should sit in a money market account) should be invested in nine to twelve months.

Case Study 2A: *Age 50 or less, married; both work, and both are ultraconservative investors.*

Money to be invested: Periodic contributions for the next ten to twenty years (see comments below if there is also a lump sum to be invested).

Even though this couple is quite conservative when it comes to investing, their equity exposure should be increased for three reasons. First, if one spouse is injured or is laid off, there will still be a paycheck coming in from the other spouse. Second, there is presumably more to invest. Third, this couple may have more investment options. For example, the husband's 401(k) plan may offer a growth portfolio but not a foreign bond account. The wife's company-sponsored plan may offer a value growth fund (a portfolio of stocks bought because their values were depressed) and a high-yield bond fund. Finally, contributions to these two retirement plans may be made at different times (such out-of-synch investments help increase time diversification and therefore reduce risk)—the husband's account may be credited on the fifteenth of every month, while the wife's plan may credit her account on the seventh.

Recommended Investments and Weightings for Each Category

30 percent	intermediate-term government bonds (bonds that mature in six to ten years)
20 percent	long-term government or corporate bond fund (maturity of over ten years)
15 percent	global equities (U.S. and foreign stocks from the major economies)

15 percent	utilities (sometimes considered boring, but usually stable and predictable)
10 percent	balanced funds (funds that invest in both stocks and bonds)
10 percent	high-yield bonds (bonds with interest payments that are about 2 percent higher than those on government bonds)

This portfolio has 65 percent of its assets in bonds and 35 percent in stocks. The overall return for this diversified portfolio should be in the 9 percent range.

If there is a lump sum to be invested (a retirement account being transferred in from a former employer), the same mix can be used, but only a third of the lump sum should be invested immediately, the second third (which should sit in a money market account) should be invested in six months and the final third should be invested in nine months.

Case Study 3A: Age 41 to 60, single, and an ultraconservative investor.

Money to be invested: Periodic contributions for the next ten to twenty-four years (see comments below if there is also a lump sum to be invested).

Since there may be as little as five years remaining until retirement, this portfolio is even more conservative. Time diversification will help reduce risk.

Recommended Investments and Weightings for Each Category

30 percent	intermediate-term government bonds (bonds that mature in six to ten years)
20 percent	long-term government or corporate bond fund (maturity of over ten years)
10 percent	short-term government or corporate bonds (maturities ranging from one to five years)
10 percent	balanced funds (funds that invest in both stocks and bonds)

10 percent	global equities (U.S. and foreign stocks from the major economies)
10 percent	high-yield bonds (bonds with interest payments that are about 2 percent higher than those on government bonds)
10 percent	utilities (sometimes considered boring, but usually stable and predictable)

This portfolio has 75 percent of its assets in bonds and 25 percent in stocks. The overall return for this diversified portfolio should be in the 7 to 8 percent range. Projected returns are brought down a little bit because of the short- and intermediate-term bond exposure.

If there is a lump sum to be invested (a retirement account being transferred in from a former employer), the same mix can be used, but only half of the lump sum should be invested immediately, the other half (which should sit in a money market account) should be invested in nine months.

Case Study 4A: Age 51 to 60, married, one or both spouses work, and both are ultraconservative investors.

Money to be invested: Periodic contributions for the next five to fifteen years (there may not be a lump sum to be rolled over from a previous retirement plan or account).

Since there may be as little as five years until retirement, the portfolio must become a little more conservative. The couple will most likely have one or more children who are either in college or about to enter a postsecondary school. Since college funds may be set up and partially funded by mom and dad, less money may be available for retirement until the kids finish school. Therefore, the recommendations below assume that less than normal contributions will be made into any kind of retirement account.

Recommended Investments and Weightings for Each Category

30 percent	intermediate-term government bonds (bonds that mature in six to ten years)
15 percent	global equities (U.S. and foreign stocks from the major economies)
15 percent	utilities (sometimes considered boring, but usually stable and predictable)
10 percent	long-term government or corporate bond fund (maturity of over ten years)
10 percent	money market fund (yields and safety are similar to bank CDs)
10 percent	balanced funds (funds that invest in both stocks and bonds)
10 percent	high-yield bonds (bonds with interest payments that are about 2 percent higher than those on government bonds)

This portfolio has 75 percent of its assets in bonds and 25 percent in stocks. The overall return for this diversified portfolio should be in the 6 to 7 percent range. Money market funds are a great risk reducer (when interest rates go up, bond prices drop, but money market yields increase). However, they do not have particularly high yields, especially once the return is adjusted for inflation.

Case Study 5A: Age 61 or older, single or married; one or both spouses work, both are ultraconservative investors, and both are expected to retire in less than five years.

Money to be invested: Periodic contributions for the next zero to four years (there may not be a lump sum to be rolled over from a previous retirement plan or account)

These ultraconservative individuals can see that retirement is in sight. Their biggest concern is stability. The cumulative effects of inflation, now or in the future, will probably not register until this individual or couple is 70 or older.

Recommended Investments and Weightings for Each Category

40 percent	intermediate-term government bonds (bonds that mature in six to ten years)
20 percent	money market fund (yields and safety are similar to bank CDs)
10 percent	global equities (U.S. and foreign stocks from the major economies)
10 percent	utilities (sometimes considered boring, but usually stable and predictable)
10 percent	balanced funds (funds that invest in both stocks and bonds)
10 percent	high-yield bonds (bonds with interest payments that are about 2 percent higher than those on government bonds)

This portfolio has 80 percent of its assets in bonds and 20 percent in stocks. The overall return for this diversified portfolio should be in the 6 to 7 percent range. Equity exposure is decreased for this portfolio since there is less remaining time to recover from a correction or a crash.

Case Study 1B: Age 40 or less, single, and a conservative investor.

Money to be invested: Periodic contributions for the next fifteen to twenty-five years (see comments below if there is also a lump sum to be invested).

Despite a low tolerance for risk, this investor should still have the bulk of his regular 401(k) contributions in equities for three reasons: First, the chances that a diversified stock portfolio (e.g., a growth fund or an index fund that closely tracks the S&P 500) will underperform a bond or money market fund over the next fifteen to twenty-five years are slim. Second, time diversification (investing money over a number of years) will greatly reduce interest-rate risk (when interest rates go up, bond prices drop, and vice versa) and market risk (the ups and downs of the stock market). Third, a combination of several different investment categories, including foreign securities, is another way to reduce risk, since these categories do not necessarily respond to the same economic or market news.

Recommended Investments and Weightings for Each Category

20 percent	balanced funds (funds that invest in both stocks and bonds)
20 percent	intermediate-term government bonds (bonds that mature in six to ten years)
15 percent	growth and income (large-company stocks, some of which have a 3 percent or higher dividend)
15 percent	high-yield bonds (bonds with interest payments that are about 2 percent higher than those on government bonds)
10 percent	growth (a portfolio of blue-chip stocks like those found in the S&P 500)
10 percent	foreign equities (large-cap stocks of companies outside of the United States)
10 percent	utilities (sometimes considered boring, but usually stable and predictable)

This portfolio has 45 percent of its assets in bonds and 55 percent in stocks. The overall return for this diversified portfolio should be in the 9 to 10 percent range. If you find the idea of owning seven different funds or subaccounts too confusing or troublesome, or if such options are not available, you can get similar results with a little less diversification by investing as follows: 45 percent in balanced funds, 25 percent in global equities (a portfolio of U.S. and foreign stocks), and 30 percent in a high-quality corporate bond fund or government securities fund (check with the management company to make sure the average maturity of the bonds in the portfolio is ten years or less).

If there is a lump sum to be invested (a retirement account

being transferred in from a former employer), the same mix can be used, but only half of the lump sum should be invested immediately; the other half (which should sit in a money market account) should be invested in six to nine months.

Case Study 2B: *Age 50 or less, married; both work, and both are conservative investors.*

Money to be invested: Periodic contributions for the next ten to twenty years (see comments below if there is also a lump sum to be invested).

There is a strong likelihood that this couple has children who may be going to college now or sometime in the future. The tendency will be to gravitate toward only debt instruments (most parents invest college funds in zero-coupon bonds, CDs, or Series EE bonds). This would be a mistake for two reasons. First, college costs outpaced inflation by 2 to 1 during the 1980s, and bonds have historically not been a good hedge against rising costs. Second, this is still a relatively young couple. The odds are that one or both of these people will live twenty-five to thirty more years.

Recommended Investments and Weightings for Each Category

20 percent	growth and income (large-company stocks, some of which have a 3 percent or higher dividend)
25 percent	balanced funds (funds that invest in both stocks and bonds)
20 percent	intermediate-term government bonds (bonds that mature in six to ten years)
15 percent	high-yield bonds (bonds with interest payments that are about 2 percent higher than those on government bonds)
10 percent	foreign equities (large-cap stocks of companies outside of the United States)
10 percent	utilities (sometimes considered boring, but usually stable and predictable)

This portfolio has 45 percent of its assets in bonds and 55 percent in stocks. The overall return for this diversified portfolio should be in the 10 percent range. If you find the idea of owning six different funds or subaccounts too confusing or troublesome, you should be able to get similar results with a little less diversification by investing as follows: 40 percent in a balanced fund, 35 percent in global equities (a portfolio of U.S. and foreign stocks), and 25 percent in a high-quality corporate bond fund or government securities fund (check with the management company to make sure the average maturity of the bonds in the portfolio is ten years or less).

If there is a lump sum to be invested (a retirement account being transferred in from a former employer), the same mix can be used, but only half of the lump sum should be invested immediately; the other half (which should sit in a money market account) should be invested in six to nine months.

Case Study 3B: Age 41 to 60, single, and a conservative investor.

Money to be invested: Periodic contributions for the next ten to twenty-four years (see comments below if there is also a lump sum to be invested).

Recommended Investments and Weightings for Each Category

20 percent	growth and income (large-company stocks, some of which have a 3 percent or higher dividend)
20 percent	balanced funds (funds that invest in both stocks and bonds)
15 percent	intermediate-term government bonds (bonds that mature in six to ten years)
15 percent	high-yield bonds (bonds with interest payments that are about 2 percent higher than those on government bonds)
15 percent	growth (a portfolio of blue-chip stocks like those found in the S&P 500)

    10 percent   foreign equities (large-cap stocks of companies outside of the
                       United States)

    5 percent   utilities (sometimes considered boring, but usually stable and
                       predictable)

This portfolio has 40 percent of its assets in bonds and 60 percent in stocks. The overall return for this diversified portfolio should be in the 10 to 11 percent range. If you do not want or cannot have this many options, you should be able to get similar results with a little less diversification by investing as follows: 50 percent in a balanced fund, 30 percent in global equities (a portfolio of U.S. and foreign stocks), and 20 percent in a high-quality corporate bond fund or government securities fund (check with the management company to make sure the average maturity of the bonds in the portfolio is ten years or less).

If there is a lump sum to be invested (a retirement account being transferred in from a former employer), the same mix can be used, but only half of the lump sum should be invested immediately; the other half (which should sit in a money market account) should be invested in six to nine months.

Case Study 4B: *Age 51 to 60, married; one or both spouses work, and both are conservative investors.*

Money to be invested: Periodic contributions for the next five to fifteen years (plus there may or may not be a lump sum to be rolled over from a previous retirement plan or account).

Since there may be as little as five years until retirement, the portfolio must be a little more conservative. The couple will most likely have one or more children who are either in college or about to enter a postsecondary school. Since college funds may be set up and partially funded by mom and dad,

less money may be available for retirement until the kids finish school. Therefore, the recommendations below assume
that less than normal contributions will be made into any kind
of retirement account.

Stocks and bonds can still be evenly represented for this
conservative couple since several categories of securities are
being included (bringing the risk level down) and because
money (at least from one spouse) is going to be added for at
least several years.

Recommended Investments and Weightings for Each Category

25 percent	growth and income (large-company stocks, some of which have a 3 percent or higher dividend)
20 percent	balanced funds (funds that invest in both stocks and bonds)
20 percent	intermediate-term government bonds (bonds that mature in six to ten years)
20 percent	high-yield bonds (bonds with interest payments that are about 2 percent higher than those on government bonds)
15 percent	foreign equities (large-cap stocks of companies outside of the United States)

This portfolio has 50 percent of its assets in bonds and 50
percent in stocks. The overall return for this diversified portfolio should be in the 10 percent range.

If there is a lump sum to be invested (a retirement account
being transferred in from a former employer), the same mix
can be used, but only half of the lump sum should be invested
immediately; the other half (which should sit in a money
market account) should be invested in six to nine months.

Case study #5B: *Age 61 or older, single or married; one or
both spouses work, and both are conservative investors.*

Money to be invested: Periodic contributions for the next

zero to four years from one or both (see comments below if there is also a lump sum to be invested).

Recommended Investments and Weightings for Each Category

35 percent	intermediate-term government bonds (bonds that mature in six to ten years)
15 percent	high-yield bonds (bonds with interest payments that are about 2 percent higher than those on government bonds)
10 percent	utilities (sometimes considered boring, but usually stable and predictable)
10 percent	growth and income (large-company stocks, some of which have a 3 percent or higher dividend)
10 percent	foreign equities (large-cap stocks of companies outside of the United States)
10 percent	international bonds (bonds issued from stable economies overseas)
10 percent	money market account

This portfolio has 70 percent of its assets in debt instruments and 30 percent in stocks. The overall return for this diversified portfolio should be in the 8 percent range.

If there is a lump sum to be invested (a retirement account being transferred in from a former employer), the same mix can be used, but only half of the lump sum should be invested immediately; the other half (which should sit in a money market account) should be invested in six to nine months.

Case Study 1C: Age 40 or less, single, and a conservative-to-moderate investor.

Money to be invested: Periodic contributions for the next fifteen to twenty-five years (see comments below if there is also a lump sum to be invested).

Despite moderate-to-conservative tolerance for risk, this

investor should put the bulk of his or her regular 401(k) contributions in equities for three reasons. First, the chances that a diversified stock portfolio (e.g., a growth fund or an index fund that closely tracks the S&P 500) will underperform a bond or money market account over the next fifteen to twenty-five years are slim. Second, time diversification (investing money over a number of years) will greatly reduce interest-rate risk (when interest rates go up, bond prices drop, and vice versa) and market risk (the ups and downs of the stock market). Third, the combination of several different investment categories, including foreign securities, is another way to reduce risk, since these categories do not necessarily respond to the same economic or market news.

Recommended Investments and Weightings for Each Category

20 percent	growth and income (large-company stocks, some of which have a 3 percent or higher dividend)
20 percent	growth (a portfolio of blue-chip stocks like those found in the S&P 500)
20 percent	foreign equities (large-cap stocks of companies outside of the United States)
15 percent	intermediate-term government bonds (bonds that mature in six to ten years)
15 percent	high-yield bonds (bonds with interest payments that are about 2 percent higher than those on government bonds)
10 percent	utilities (sometimes considered boring, but usually stable and predictable)

This portfolio has 30 percent of its assets in bonds and 70 percent in stocks. The overall return for this diversified conservative-to-moderate portfolio should be in the 10 to 11 percent range. If not all of these investment options are available to you, a similar risk-adjusted return can be obtained by investing 60 percent in a balanced fund (or variable annuity subaccount) and 40 percent in a global stock fund.

If there is a lump sum to be invested (a retirement account being transferred in from a former employer), the same mix can be used, but only half of the lump sum should be invested immediately; the other half (which should sit in a money market account) should be invested in six to nine months.

Case Study 2C: Age 50 or less, married; both work, and both are conservative-to-moderate investors.

Money to be invested: Periodic contributions for the next ten to twenty years (see comments below if there is also a lump sum to be invested).

There is a strong likelihood that this couple has children who may be going to college now or sometime in the future. The tendency will be to gravitate toward only debt instruments (most parents invest college funds in zero-coupon bonds, CDs, or Series EE bonds). This would be a mistake for two reasons. First, college costs outpaced inflation by 2 to 1 during the 1980s, and bonds have historically not been a good hedge against rising costs. Second, this is still a relatively young couple. The odds are that one or both of these people will live twenty-five to thirty more years.

Recommended Investments and Weightings for Each Category

25 percent	growth and income (large-company stocks, some of which have a 3 percent or higher dividend)
20 percent	growth (a portfolio of blue-chip stocks like those found in the S&P 500)
20 percent	foreign equities (large-cap stocks of companies outside of the United States)
15 percent	intermediate-term government bonds (bonds that mature in six to ten years)

10 percent	high-yield bonds (bonds with interest payments that are about 2 percent higher than those on government bonds)
10 percent	utilities (sometimes considered boring, but usually stable and predictable)

This portfolio has 25 percent of its assets in bonds and 75 percent in stocks. The overall return for this portfolio should be in the 11 percent range. If not all of these investment options are available to you, a similar risk-adjusted return can be obtained by investing 55 percent in a balanced fund (or variable annuity subaccount) and 45 percent in a global stock fund.

If there is a lump sum to be invested (a retirement account being transferred in from a former employer), the same mix can be used, but only half of the lump sum should be invested immediately; the other half (which should sit in a money market account) should be invested in six to nine months.

Case Study 3C: Age 41 to 60, single, and a conservative-to-moderate investor.

Money to be invested: Periodic contributions for the next ten to twenty-four years (see comments below if there is also a lump sum to be invested).

Recommended Investments and Weightings for Each Category

20 percent	growth and income (large-company stocks, some of which have a 3 percent or higher dividend)
20 percent	high-yield bonds (bonds with interest payments that are about 2 percent higher than those on government bonds)
20 percent	foreign equities (large-cap stocks of companies outside of the United States)
15 percent	intermediate-term government bonds (bonds that mature in six to ten years)

| 15 percent | growth (a portfolio of blue-chip stocks like those found in the S&P 500) |
| 10 percent | utilities (sometimes considered boring, but usually stable and predictable) |

This portfolio has 35 percent of its assets in bonds and 65 percent in stocks. The overall return for this portfolio should be in the 10 percent range. If not all of these investment options are available to you, a similar risk-adjusted return can be obtained by investing 70 percent in a balanced fund (or variable annuity subaccount) and 30 percent in a global stock fund.

If there is a lump sum to be invested (a retirement account being transferred in from a former employer), the same mix can be used, but only half of the lump sum should be invested immediately; the other half (which should sit in a money market account) should be invested in six to nine months.

Case Study 4C: Age 51 to 60, married; one or both spouses work, and both are conservative-to-moderate investors.

Money to be invested: Periodic contributions for the next five to fifteen years (plus there may or may not be a lump sum to be rolled over from a previous retirement plan or account).

Since there may be as little as five years until retirement, debt instruments will play a more important role.

Recommended Investments and Weightings for Each Category

| 20 percent | growth and income (large-company stocks, some of which have a 3 percent or higher dividend) |
| 20 percent | high-yield bonds (bonds with interest payments that are about 2 percent higher than those on government bonds) |

20 percent	intermediate-term government bonds (bonds that mature in six to ten years)
15 percent	foreign equities (large-cap stocks of companies outside of the United States)
15 percent	growth (a portfolio of blue-chip stocks like those found in the S&P 500)
10 percent	utilities (sometimes considered boring, but usually stable and predictable)

This portfolio has 40 percent of its assets in bonds and 60 percent in stocks. The overall return for this portfolio should be in the 9 to 10 percent range. If not all of these investment options are available to you, a similar risk-adjusted return can be obtained by investing 80 percent in a balanced fund (or variable annuity subaccount) and 20 percent in a global stock fund.

If there is a lump sum to be invested (a retirement account being transferred in from a former employer), the same mix can be used, but only half of the lump sum should be invested immediately; the other half (which should sit in a money market account) should be invested in six to nine months.

Case Study 5C: Age 61 or older, single or married; one or both spouses work, and both are conservative-to-moderate investors.

Money to be invested: Periodic contributions for the next zero to four years from one or both (see comments below if there is also a lump sum to be invested).

Retirement may be just around the corner. Therefore this portfolio will be weighted slightly more than usual towards bonds. At this stage in life, the conservative-to-moderate individual or couple becomes a little less concerned with return and inflation and more concerned with predictability. The

assurances become even more important if they are supporting one or more children.

Recommended Investments and Weightings for Each Category

25 percent	intermediate-term government bonds (bonds that mature in six to ten years)
20 percent	growth and income (large-company stocks, some of which have a 3 percent or higher dividend)
20 percent	high-yield bonds (bonds with interest payments that are about 2 percent higher than those on government bonds)
15 percent	foreign equities (large-cap stocks of companies outside of the United States)
10 percent	growth (a portfolio of blue-chip stocks like those found in the S&P 500)
10 percent	utilities (sometimes considered boring, but usually stable and predictable)

This portfolio has 45 percent of its assets in bonds and 55
percent in stocks. The overall return for this portfolio should
be in the 9 to 10 percent range. If not all of these investment
options are available to you, a similar risk-adjusted return can
be obtained by investing 85 percent in a balanced fund (or
variable annuity subaccount) and 15 percent in a global stock
fund.

If there is a lump sum to be invested (a retirement account
being transferred in from a former employer), the same mix
can be used, but only half of the lump sum should be invested
immediately; the other half (which should sit in a money
market account) should be invested in six months.

Case Study 1D: Age 40 or less, single, and a moderate investor.

Money to be invested: Periodic contributions for the next

fifteen to twenty-five years (see comments below if there is also a lump sum to be invested).

Despite having only a moderate tolerance for risk, this investor should still put the bulk of his or her regular 401(k) contributions in equities for three reasons. First, the chances that a diversified stock portfolio (e.g., a growth fund or an index fund that closely tracks the S&P 500) will underperform a bond or money market account over the next fifteen to twenty-five years are slim. Second, time diversification (investing money over a number of years) will greatly reduce interest-rate risk (when interest rates go up, bond prices drop, and vice versa) and market risk (the ups and downs of the stock market). Third, the combination of several different investment categories, including foreign securities, is another way to reduce risk, since these categories do not necessarily respond to the same economic or market news.

Recommended Investments and Weightings for Each Category

25 percent	growth and income (large-company stocks, some of which have a 3 percent or higher dividend)
20 percent	growth (a portfolio of blue-chip stocks like those found in the S&P 500)
20 percent	foreign equities (large-cap stocks of companies outside of the United States)
10 percent	aggressive growth (stocks whose market capitalization is less than $1 billion)
15 percent	high-yield bonds (bonds with interest payments that are about 2 percent higher than those on government bonds)
10 percent	utilities (sometimes considered boring, but usually stable and predictable)

This portfolio has 15 percent of its assets in bonds and 85 percent in stocks. The overall return for this diversified moderate portfolio should be in the 12 to 13 percent range. If not all of these investment options are available to you, a similar risk-adjusted return can be obtained by investing 60 percent in a growth and income fund and 40 percent in a global stock fund.

If there is a lump sum to be invested (a retirement account being transferred in from a former employer), the same mix can be used, but only half of the lump sum should be invested immediately; the other half (which should sit in a money market account) should be invested in six months.

Case Study 2D: *Age 50 or less, married; both work, and both are moderate investors.*

Money to be invested: Periodic contributions for the next ten to twenty years (see comments below if there is also a lump sum to be invested).

Recommended Investments and Weightings for Each Category

25 percent	growth and income (large-company stocks, some of which have a 3 percent or higher dividend)
25 percent	foreign equities (large-cap stocks of companies outside of the United States)
20 percent	growth (a portfolio of blue-chip stocks like those found in the S&P 500)
10 percent	aggressive growth (stocks whose market capitalization is less than $1 billion)
10 percent	high-yield bonds (bonds with interest payments that are about 2 percent higher than those on government bonds)
10 percent	utilities (sometimes considered boring, but usually stable and predictable)

This portfolio has 20 percent of its assets in debt instruments and 80 percent in stocks. The overall return for this diversified moderate portfolio should be in the 12 to 13 percent range. If not all of these investment options are available to you, a similar risk-adjusted return can be obtained by investing 50 percent in a growth and income fund and 50 percent in a global stock fund.

If there is a lump sum to be invested (a retirement account being transferred in from a former employer), the same mix can be used, but only half of the lump sum should be invested immediately; the other half (which should sit in a money market account) should be invested in six to nine months.

Case Study 3D: *Age 41 to 60, single, and a moderate investor.*

Money to be invested: Periodic contributions for the next ten to twenty-four years (see comments below if there is also a lump sum to be invested).

Recommended Investments and Weightings for Each Category

25 percent	foreign equities (large-cap stocks of companies outside of the United States)
20 percent	growth and income (large-company stocks, some of which have a 3 percent or higher dividend)
20 percent	growth (a portfolio of blue-chip stocks like those found in the S&P 500)
10 percent	aggressive growth (stocks whose market capitalization is less than $1 billion)
25 percent	high-yield bonds (bonds with interest payments that are about 2 percent higher than those on government bonds)

This portfolio has 25 percent of its assets in bonds and 75 percent in stocks. The overall return for this diversified moderate portfolio should be in the 11 to 12 percent range. If not all of these investment options are available to you, a similar risk-adjusted return can be obtained by investing 75 percent in a global stock fund and 25 percent in a corporate bond fund.

If there is a lump sum to be invested (a retirement account being transferred in from a former employer), the same mix can be used, but only half of the lump sum should be invested immediately; the other half (which should sit in a money market account) should be invested in twelve months.

Case Study 4D: *Age 51 to 60, married; one or both spouses work, and both are moderate investors.*

Money to be invested: Periodic contributions for the next five to fifteen years (plus there may or may not be a lump sum to be rolled over from a previous retirement plan or account).

Since there may be as little as five years until retirement, debt instruments will play a more important role.

Recommended Investments and Weightings for Each Category

25 percent	growth and income (large-company stocks, some of which have a 3 percent or higher dividend)
25 percent	foreign equities (large-cap stocks of companies outside of the United States)
20 percent	growth (a portfolio of blue-chip stocks like those found in the S&P 500)
10 percent	aggressive growth (stocks whose market capitalization is less than $1 billion)
10 percent	high-yield bonds (bonds with interest payments that are about 2 percent higher than those on government bonds)
10 percent	cash (money market account or CDs maturing in one year or less)

This portfolio has 20 percent of its assets in debt instruments and 80 percent in stocks. The overall return for this diversified moderate portfolio should be in the 11 to 12 percent range. If all of these investment options are not available to you, a similar risk-adjusted return can be obtained by investing 40 percent in a growth fund, 50 percent in a global stock fund, and 10 percent in a money market account.

If there is a lump sum to be invested (a retirement account being transferred in from a former employer), the same mix can be used, but only half of the lump sum should be invested immediately; the other half (which should sit in a money market account) should be invested in six to nine months.

Case Study 5D: *Age 61 or older, single or married; one or both spouses work, and both are moderate investors.*

Money to be invested: Periodic contributions for the next zero to four years from one or both (see comments below if there is also a lump sum to be invested).

Retirement may be just around the corner. Therefore, this portfolio will be weighted slightly more than usual towards bonds. At this stage in life, the moderate individual or couple becomes a little less concerned with return and inflation and more concerned with predictability. These assurances become even more important if they are supporting one or more children.

Recommended Investments and Weightings for Each Category

20 percent	growth and income (large-company stocks, some of which have a 3 percent or higher dividend)
20 percent	foreign equities (large-cap stocks of companies outside of the United States)
20 percent	growth (a portfolio of blue-chip stocks like those found in the S&P 500)

15 percent	high-yield bonds (bonds with interest payments that are about 2 percent higher than those on government bonds)
15 percent	cash (money market account or CDs maturing in one year or less)
10 percent	aggressive growth (stocks whose market capitalization is less than $1 billion)

This portfolio has 30 percent of its assets in debt instruments and 70 percent in stocks. The overall return for this diversified moderate portfolio should be in the 11 percent range. If not all of these investment options are available to you, a similar risk-adjusted return can be obtained by investing 40 percent in a growth fund, 50 percent in a global stock fund, and 10 percent in a money market account.

If there is a lump sum to be invested (a retirement account being transferred in from a former employer), the same mix can be used, but only a third of the lump sum should be invested immediately; another third can be invested in nine months, and the final third invested in sixteen months.

Case Study 1E: *Age 40 or less, single, and a fairly aggressive investor.*

Money to be invested: Periodic contributions for the next fifteen to twenty-five years (see comments below if there is also a lump sum to be invested).

Recommended Investments and Weightings for Each Category

35 percent	foreign equities (large-cap stocks of companies outside of the United States)
25 percent	growth (a portfolio of blue-chip stocks like those found in the S&P 500)
25 percent	aggressive growth (stocks whose market capitalization is less than $1 billion)

15 percent	growth and income (large-company stocks, some of which have a 3 percent or higher dividend)

This portfolio is 100 percent in stocks. The overall return for this fairly aggressive portfolio should be in the 15 percent range.

If there is a lump sum to be invested (a retirement account being transferred in from a former employer), the same mix can be used, but only half of the lump sum should be invested immediately; the other half (which should sit in a money market account) should be invested in six months.

Case Study 2E: Age 50 or less, married, both work, and both are fairly aggressive investors.

Money to be invested: Periodic contributions for the next ten to twenty years (see comments below if there is also a lump sum to be invested).

Recommended Investments and Weightings for Each Category

30 percent	foreign equities (large-cap stocks of companies outside of the United States)
25 percent	growth (a portfolio of blue-chip stocks like those found in the S&P 500)
20 percent	aggressive growth (stocks whose market capitalization is less than $1 billion)
25 percent	growth and income (large-company stocks, some of which have a 3 percent or higher dividend)

This portfolio is 100 percent in stocks. The overall return for this fairly aggressive portfolio should be in the 14 percent range.

If there is a lump sum to be invested (a retirement account being transferred in from a former employer), the same mix can be used, but only half of the lump sum should be invested immediately; the other half (which should sit in a money market account) should be invested in six to nine months.

Case Study 3E: *Age 41 to 60, single, and a fairly aggressive investor.*

Money to be invested: Periodic contributions for the next ten to twenty-four years (see comments below if there is also a lump sum to be invested).

Recommended Investments and Weightings for Each Category

30 percent	foreign equities (large-cap stocks of companies outside of the United States)
30 percent	growth and income (large-company stocks, some of which have a 3 percent or higher dividend)
20 percent	growth (a portfolio of blue-chip stocks like those found in the S&P 500)
20 percent	aggressive growth (stocks whose market capitalization is less than $1 billion)

This portfolio is 100 percent in stocks. The overall return for this fairly aggressive portfolio should be in the 13 to 14 percent range.

If there is a lump sum to be invested (a retirement account being transferred in from a former employer), the same mix can be used, but only half of the lump sum should be invested immediately; the other half (which should sit in a money market account) should be invested in twelve months.

Case Study 4E: *Age 51 to 60, married; one or both spouses work, and both are fairly aggressive investors.*

Money to be invested: Periodic contributions for the next five to fifteen years (plus there may or may not be a lump sum to be rolled over from a previous retirement plan or account).

Even though there may be as little as five years until retirement, debt instruments should still not be part of a fairly aggressive portfolio. More often than not, such investments tend to lower returns.

Recommended Investments and Weightings for Each Category

25 percent	foreign equities (large-cap stocks of companies outside of the United States)
25 percent	growth and income (large-company stocks, some of which have a 3 percent or higher dividend)
20 percent	growth (a portfolio of blue-chip stocks like those found in the S&P 500)
15 percent	aggressive growth (stocks whose market capitalization is less than $1 billion)
15 percent	utilities (sometimes considered boring, but usually stable and predictable)

This portfolio is 100 percent in stocks. The overall return for this fairly aggressive portfolio should be in the 13 percent range.

If there is a lump sum to be invested (a retirement account being transferred in from a former employer), the same mix can be used, but only half of the lump sum should be invested immediately; the other half (which should sit in a money market account) should be invested in twelve months.

Case Study 5E: Age 61 or older, single or married; one or both spouses work, and both are fairly aggressive investors.

Money to be invested: Periodic contributions for the next zero to four years from one or both (see comments below if there is also a lump sum to be invested).

Retirement may be just around the corner. Therefore this portfolio will include cash. At this stage in life, even fairly aggressive individuals or couples become a little less concerned with return and inflation and more concerned with predictability. These assurances become even more important if they are supporting one or more children.

Recommended Investments and Weightings for Each Category

25 percent	foreign equities (large-cap stocks of companies outside of the United States)
20 percent	growth and income (large-company stocks, some of which have a 3 percent or higher dividend)
20 percent	growth (a portfolio of blue-chip stocks like those found in the S&P 500)
10 percent	aggressive growth (stocks whose market capitalization is less than $1 billion)
15 percent	utilities (sometimes considered boring, but usually stable and predictable)
10 percent	cash (money market account or CDs maturing in one year or less)

This portfolio is 90 percent in stocks and 10 percent in cash. The overall return for this fairly aggressive portfolio should be in the 12 to 13 percent range.

If there is a lump sum to be invested (a retirement account being transferred in from a former employer), the same mix can be used, but only a third of the lump sum should be invested immediately; another third can be invested in nine months, and the final third invested in sixteen months.

Case Study 1F: Age 40 or less, single, and an aggressive investor.

Money to be invested: Periodic contributions for the next

fifteen to twenty-five years (see comments below if there is also a lump sum to be invested).

Recommended Investments and Weightings for Each Category

40 percent	aggressive growth (stocks whose market capitalization is less than $1 billion)
40 percent	foreign equities (large-cap stocks of companies outside of the United States)
20 percent	growth (a portfolio of blue-chip stocks like those found in the S&P 500)

This portfolio is 100 percent in stocks. The overall return for this aggressive portfolio should be in the 16 percent range.

If there is a lump sum to be invested (a retirement account being transferred in from a former employer), the same mix can be used, but only half of the lump sum should be invested immediately; the other half (which should sit in a money market account) should be invested in six months.

Case Study 2F: *Age 50 or less, married, both work, and both are aggressive investors.*

Money to be invested: Periodic contributions for the next ten to twenty years (see comments below if there is also a lump sum to be invested).

Recommended Investments and Weightings for Each Category

35 percent	aggressive growth (stocks whose market capitalization is less than $1 billion)
35 percent	foreign equities (large-cap stocks of companies outside of the United States)
20 percent	growth (a portfolio of blue-chip stocks like those found in the S&P 500)

| 10 percent | growth and income (large-company stocks, some of which have a 3 percent or higher dividend) |

This portfolio is 100 percent in stocks. The overall return for this aggressive portfolio should be in the 15 percent range.

If there is a lump sum to be invested (a retirement account being transferred in from a former employer), the same mix can be used, but only half of the lump sum should be invested immediately; the other half (which should sit in a money market account) should be invested in six to nine months.

Case Study 3F: *Age 41 to 60, single, and an aggressive investor.*

Money to be invested: Periodic contributions for the next ten to twenty-four years (see comments below if there is also a lump sum to be invested).

Recommended Investments and Weightings for Each Category

40 percent	foreign equities (large-cap stocks of companies outside of the United States)
30 percent	aggressive growth (stocks whose market capitalization is less than $1 billion)
20 percent	growth (a portfolio of blue-chip stocks like those found in the S&P 500)
10 percent	growth and income (large-company stocks, some of which have a 3 percent or higher dividend)

This portfolio is 100 percent in stocks. The overall return for this aggressive portfolio should be in the 15 percent range.

If there is a lump sum to be invested (a retirement account being transferred in from a former employer), the same mix can be used, but only half of the lump sum should be invested immediately; the other half (which should sit in a money market account) should be invested in twelve months.

Case Study 4F: Age 51 to 60, married, one or both spouses work, and both are aggressive investors.

Money to be invested: Periodic contributions for the next five to fifteen years (plus there may or may not be a lump sum to be rolled over from a previous retirement plan or account).

Even though there may be as little as five years until retirement, debt instruments should still not be part of an aggressive portfolio. More often than not, such investments tend to lower returns.

Recommended Investments and Weightings for Each Category

35 percent	foreign equities (large-cap stocks of companies outside of the United States)
30 percent	aggressive growth (stocks whose market capitalization is less than $1 billion)
15 percent	growth (a portfolio of blue-chip stocks like those found in the S&P 500)
10 percent	growth and income (large-company stocks, some of which have a 3 percent or higher dividend)
10 percent	utilities (sometimes considered boring, but usually stable and predictable)

This portfolio is 100 percent in stocks. The overall return for this aggressive portfolio should be in the 14 to 15 percent range.

If there is a lump sum to be invested (a retirement account being transferred in from a former employer), the same mix can be used, but only half of the lump sum should be invested immediately; the other half (which should sit in a money market account) should be invested in six to nine months.

Case Study 5F: *Age 61 or older, single or married, one or both spouses work, and both are aggressive investors.*

Money to be invested: Periodic contributions for the next zero to four years from one or both (see comments below if there is also a lump sum to be invested).

Retirement may be just around the corner. Therefore this portfolio will be weighed slightly more than usual towards bonds. At this stage in life, even an aggressive investor becomes a little less concerned with return and inflation and more concerned with predictability. These assurances become even more important if they are supporting one or more children.

Recommended Investments and Weightings for Each Category

30 percent	foreign equities (large-cap stocks of companies outside of the United States)
25 percent	aggressive growth (stocks whose market capitalization is less than $1 billion)
15 percent	growth (a portfolio of blue-chip stocks like those found in the S&P 500)
10 percent	growth and income (large-company stocks, some of which have a 3 percent or higher dividend)
10 percent	utilities (sometimes considered boring, but usually stable and predictable)
10 percent	cash (money market account or CDs maturing in one year or less)

This portfolio is 90 percent in stocks and 10 percent in cash. The overall return for this aggressive portfolio should be in the 13 to 14 percent range.

If there is a lump sum to be invested (a retirement account

being transferred in from a former employer), the same mix can be used, but only a third of the lump sum should be invested immediately; another third can be invested in nine months, and the final third invested in sixteen months.

CHAPTER 8
Investing in Debt Instruments

As you may recall from an earlier chapter, a debt instrument represents any investment in which you lend your money to someone else. Debt instruments offer either a fixed rate of return for a specific period of time (e.g., a bank CD that pays you 6 percent for one year) or a rate that changes with the general level of interest rates (e.g., a money market account).

There are a great number of debt instruments that you can invest in; however, when it comes to 401(k) plans, the number is usually quite limited. Still, the options available under many plans are extensive enough for the great majority of employees. This chapter covers seven of the most common investment choices (for debt instruments) within a 401(k) plan. Those investment options are certificates of deposit (CDs), money market funds, high-quality corporate bonds, fixed-rate annuities, zero-coupon bonds, high-yield bond funds, and foreign bonds.

As a participant in a 401(k) plan, it is very likely that you will be offered these debt instruments through a mutual fund or variable annuity. So, instead of being able to buy General Motors bonds, for example, you would invest in the XYZ Corporate Bond Fund or the ABC Variable Annuity Subaccount, which includes a number of different bonds with different maturities and somewhat different interest rates (or

yields). The portfolio offered to you may not include General
Motors bonds, but it will include a great number of bonds that
will go up and down in value just like GM bonds and have
approximately the same yield.

The advantage of going into a portfolio (a mutual fund or
variable annuity subaccount or variable life insurance account)
is that you have instant diversification. You no longer have to
worry about whether Chrysler, IBM, or any other single company will go bankrupt or suffer from negative financial news.
Instead, you will own part of a portfolio that might own fifty
to two hundred different bonds. This is a much safer way to
own the kinds of investments you like, without sacrificing performance. Furthermore, the actual buying and selling of these
securities can be less expensive, meaning that your net return
can end up being higher. Finally, when packaged products
such as mutual funds and variable annuities are used, the costs
to your employer are lower, making it more likely that your
boss will continue to offer a 401(k) or other retirement plan.

Each of the following discussions begins with a table that
summarizes the volatility and total return potential, as well as
the recommended holding period for the specific investment.

Volatility refers to how risky the investment is; it has to do
with the range of returns that are most likely to be experienced. An investment that could be up 15 percent one year
and down 10 percent the next year is obviously much riskier,
and less predictable, than one that might be up 5 percent one
year and down 6 percent the following year. The lower the
volatility, the safer the investment. A moderate or high level of
volatility does not mean that this is a somewhat or outright
risky investment that should be avoided. It all depends upon
your time horizon and your tolerance for risk. (A number of
"risky" investments become quite safe if they are owned for
five years or more, so that the extremes cancel each other out.)

Total return potential shows you what you can expect when it comes to a return on your investment. "Total return" is calculated by taking any interest or dividends paid by the investment and adding it to any price appreciation. As an example, if a high-yield bond pays 8 percent in interest and the price per share of the high-yield bond portfolio increases from $10 to $11 a share, your total return would be 18 percent (the 8 percent interest plus the 10 percent price per share appreciation). If the same high-yield bond fund pays 8 percent but the price per share drops from $10 to $9 a share (a 10 percent drop in principal), the total return becomes -2 percent (8 percent *minus* 10 percent).

If the investment you are reading about has a total return potential that is "poor to fair," this means that once inflation is subtracted, the real return on the investment is probably in the 0 to 2 percent range. This does not mean that the investment should be avoided by everyone. Typically investments with *real returns* (meaning returns adjusted for inflation and eventually income taxes) that are zero or positive by only one or two percentage points are appropriate for consideration by a conservative investor (or a moderate to aggressive investor who is simply looking for a place to temporarily park her money until a buying opportunity arises).

Recommended holding period offers a general suggestion as to how long you should own the investment. As an example, the recommended holding period for certificates of deposit (the first investment described below) is "0-1 year." This means that CDs should not really be considered an *investment*, but instead a place to park money until there is a stock market correction, interest rates start to head down (making bonds an attractive choice), or you become more familiar and comfortable with other types of investments. At the other extreme, if the recommended holding period is five years or more, your first-year experience could be quite good or fairly bad. A recommended holding period of several years means that this is not the kind of investment you should get overly excited or depressed about based on one or two years' worth of results.

CERTIFICATES OF DEPOSIT

Volatility	Very low
Total return potential	Poor to fair
Recommended holding period	0-1 year

Certificates of deposit, more commonly referred to as CDs, represent a deposit with a bank or savings and loan association. The depositor (investor) agrees to deposit his or her money with a financial institution in return for receiving a set rate of return. The yield, or return, depends upon the amount of money being deposited, the term of the deposit, the general level of interest rates, and the competitiveness of the institution. At the end of the term, the lender (you) is free to either liquidate the entire account, principal and accumulated interest, or roll the maturing CD over into another CD for another term. The renewal rate may be higher than, lower than, or identical to the previous rate.

Whenever one thinks of bank CDs, the first things that come to mind are safety and a known rate of return. When the bank offers you a certain rate of return, you get that rate, no matter what happens to the bank's investment portfolio, the economy, or your specific dollars. If you do not like the rate of return being offered, you are always free to shop elsewhere, getting quotes and yields from other banks or savings and loan associations.

There are two possible disadvantages to investing your money in CDs. First, if you make a withdrawal before the CD matures, you may have to pay a penalty. The amount of the penalty depends upon the CD's interest rate and the financial institution. The second potential disadvantage could also end up being a positive. That is, when you lock in a set rate of return, you will know only after the fact whether your investment performed better or worse than a comparable investment that paid a floating rate, such as a money market account or adjustable-rate mortgage fund.

In theory, there is also a distant chance that your financial institution will run into trouble. Therefore, when you invest in a CD, make sure it is backed by the FDIC.

As CDs are one of America's most popular investments, it is difficult to say that they are something that should not be included in a portfolio. Yet, for most people, there are better alternatives. During periods when interest rates are rising, money market funds are a better choice (there are no penalties, and your rate of return will go up as the general level of rates increases). When interest rates seem to be stable, or even dropping, then short-term bond funds or short-term global income funds are a better choice. Their return is often several percentage points higher than that offered by CDs, and again, there is no penalty for a "premature" withdrawal.

401(k) Considerations

Certificates of deposit are not usually an option within a 401(k) plan. However, since a large number of money market funds (see the next section) have a percentage of their assets in CDs, you can participate somewhat indirectly. Bank CDs are an adequate choice for the ultraconservative 401(k) participant who does not ever want to see a decline in value on his or her statement but understands that on an after-inflation basis (and after the eventual taxation when the retirement account is liquidated), this is not a very good choice. If you are determined to include certificates of deposit as part of your overall holdings, then a 401(k) is a good place for this investment, since you will be sheltered from current income taxes.

MONEY MARKET FUNDS

Volatility	Very low
Total return potential	Poor to fair
Recommended holding period	0-1 year

Money market funds are a type of mutual fund that invests in short-term debt instruments. The types of assets include U.S. Treasury bills, CDs, Eurodollar CDs, and commercial paper. In order for a fund to be called a "money market" fund, at least 95 percent of its assets must be invested in securities that are rated extremely safe. The typical maturity of the average money market fund fluctuates from twenty-five to sixty-five days; each portfolio has some securities maturing within a few days, weeks, and months. As the "paper" matures, fund managers reinvest it in other short-term instruments immediately. No money market fund manager wants portfolio money sitting around idly, even for a day.

When you invest in a money market fund, your money is commingled with everyone else's. Each investor, whether seasoned or new, gets the same yield. If the quoted yield is, say, 5.01 percent, you will get that rate, just like an investor who has been with the fund for several years (and got a much higher or lower rate years earlier).

Money market accounts have a perfect track record: No one has ever lost a dime in one of these funds (One fund did lose money in 1995, but this was a money market account set up by a bank and most of the investors were other banks.). In addition to being extremely safe, the rate of return stays competitive with the general level of interest rates; as rates climb, so do money market yields, and vice versa. Finally, these funds are extremely liquid and marketable. Money can be added or taken out at any time.

Their rate of return has consistently been higher than that offered by U.S. Treasury Bills and interest-bearing checking and savings accounts. Like interest rates in general, the return that money market funds have provided has been all over the board in the past 20 years, ranging anywhere from just under 4 percent in the early 1990s to close to 20 percent during the very early 1980s. Usually, but not always, money market funds have also had yields that have surpassed those offered by certificates of deposit.

There is only one disadvantage with money market funds: The rate of return is not guaranteed and fluctuates from month to month, sometimes from day to day. This is not a disadvantage to most investors.

Money market funds are the perfect place to invest a large portion of the money you want to keep liquid. This is also a good "safe haven" in which to park your assets during periods of economic uncertainty or disaster. Everyone should have part of his or her portfolio in a money market fund, if for no other reason than as a means to be able to get your hands on cash in a hurry. Not only does this give one peace of mind, it is also a good source to tap when it comes time to pay monthly bills and for emergencies.

401(k) Considerations

As odd as it might sound, for the very conservative investor, a money market fund is probably a better choice than a bank CD. A CD investor who locks in a set rate of return for a set period of time, ranging from several days up to ten years, is effectively betting on interest rates. For example, if you thought rates were going to go down, you would purchase a long-term CD and preserve a high rate of return; if you thought rates were headed upward, you would stick with short-term CDs, continuously rolling over the CD as it matured into a higher-yielding CD. With a money market fund, there is no need to bet. If rates do go up, a money market fund will start to yield more; if rates decline, the same fund will slowly lower its return.

Chances are that your 401(k) will include a money market portfolio as an option as part of either a mutual fund group, a variable annuity family, or a variable life account. A money market account is a great place to be when stocks and bonds are declining or when you are uncertain about where your retirement dollars should be invested. However, like bank CDs, this investment should not be considered a place to park money for more than a year or two—under most conditions, the time period should be limited to several months or less.

Your decision as to how much of your portfolio should be invested in a money market fund should depend upon such things as whether or not: (1) you are anticipating a large purchase, such as an automobile, during the coming year, (2) the security of your job and/or that of your spouse's, (3) major lifestyle changes are on the horizon (e.g., having a baby, remodeling the home, going back to school, going through a divorce, moving, etc.) or (4) you have a negative outlook about real estate, stocks, and/or bonds.

HIGH-QUALITY CORPORATE BONDS

Volatility	Low to moderate
Total return potential	Fair
Recommended holding period	1-4 years

When a corporation issues bonds it must decide whether or not to have its security(s) rated. What distinguishes a high-quality bond from other types of corporate bonds is its rating. A good rating will make the bond more marketable. The two major rating services, Moody's and Standard & Poor's, consider the top four categories (AAA, AA, A, and Baa in the case of Moody's; AAA, AA, A, and BBB in the case of S&P) to be high quality. The higher the rating, the more likely it is that the corporation will be able to meet its current and future debt obligations. Similarly, the higher the rating, the lower the risk and the lower the yield. As the chance for default or suspension of interest payments decreases, so does the risk. The default rate for high-quality corporate bonds is a small fraction of 1 percent.

Corporations strive for a high rating because the interest paid out by the company (a cost of doing business) can amount to a large percentage of its overall expenses. A higher rating means that the company will pay less in interest if it issues new bonds in the future. A difference of one or two percentage points can end up saving, or costing, the corporation hundreds of thousands of dollars per year. The figure could turn out to be millions if the debt about to be issued amounts to a couple of hundred million dollars.

Once you buy a bond, its coupon rate (the amount of interest paid out by the corporation) is fixed. The advantage of buying a high-quality corporate bond is peace of mind. By buying a safe corporate bond, you will be getting a return that is 1 to 2 percent higher than that of a U.S. government obligation that has a similar maturity. Like other types of bonds, high-quality issues pay interest semiannually. And, like other bonds, if interest rates decline from the time when you purchased your bonds, the bonds' value will increase.

The biggest disadvantage of these bonds is that their rating can go down, thereby decreasing their value if you were to sell the bond before maturity. True, the rating may also go up, but when you have a bond that is already A or AA rated, its safety can go up only marginally, while the potential fall could be severe. Fortunately, rating adjustments are more the exception than the rule. Furthermore, the chances that a bond's rating will drop by two or more grades are slim.

The track record of high-quality corporate issues is similar to that of U.S. government securities. From 1975 to 1981, long-term bonds lost almost half of their value. During the 1980s and early 1990s, corporate bonds saw substantial appreciation. By the late 1980s, the losses incurred during the late 1970s had been wiped out.

If interest rates remain level during the 1990s, then bonds, bond funds, and unit trusts should be safe, displaying only modest changes in price. However, if there are wide swings in interest rates during the decade, all bonds, including high-quality issues, could end up being more volatile than stocks. If you anticipate such changes in interest rates, stick with bonds, funds, and unit trusts whose maturities average seven years or less. Such maturities are considered to be short- to intermediate-term, and the bonds do not change drastically in price.

Bonds are an important part of one's holdings. Often, they can add a great deal of stability when the stock or real estate market is uncertain. It is very uncommon for both high-quality bonds and stocks to decline in value the same year.

One of the nice features of high-quality corporate bonds is that they pay interest whether or not the economy, real estate, or the stock market is performing well. High-quality issues provide a reliable source of income.

401(k) Considerations

Since most company retirement plans have limited investment choices, most likely you will be able to invest in corporate bonds only via a mutual fund, variable annuity subaccount, or variable life account. This type of investment will be easy to spot, as the portfolio's name will include words such as "income," "bond," or "corporate."

Even though corporate bonds are considered riskier than government securities with similar maturity, there is little difference in yield (current income) or total return (yield plus principal appreciation or depreciation). Even though defaults are rare with good-quality corporate bonds or high-quality corporate bond funds, you may be better off accepting a little less yield with the possibility of getting a higher total return. In some situations, there is a "flight to quality" as stocks and certain kinds of bonds are abandoned as people buy government obligations—thereby making these obligations appreciate in value.

Most investors will be better served by owning U.S. government bonds. The desired maturity of any bond depends upon your circumstances and whether you feel that interest rates are going to go up or down during your period of ownership. Since there is usually little difference between the yield on government and high-quality corporate bonds with similar maturities, take the safer investment. With government securities you never have to worry about a downgrading, payment of interest, or repayment of principal.

FIXED-RATE ANNUITIES

Volatility	Very low
Total return potential	Fair
Recommended holding period	0-2 years

A fixed-rate annuity is a contractual relationship between the investor (you) and an insurance company, similar to the relationship between you and a bank when you invest in a CD. For the ability to use your money, the insurance company gives you a set rate of return for a specified period, usually one, three, or five years. At the end of the contract, you are free to withdraw part or all of your money, transfer it to another annuity issuer, or "roll it over" with the same company, accepting the then current rate of return. Money taken out of an annuity prior to its contract expiration date may be subject to a penalty. With most companies, this penalty cannot eat into your principal.

Money invested in an annuity grows and compounds tax-deferred, making this a somewhat unique investment vehicle. Fixed-rate annuities are also one of the few investments you can go into in which your principal is guaranteed each and every day.

There are three reasons why people buy fixed-rate annuities inside a 401(k) plan: (1) their principal and interest are safe, (2) they receive a specific rate of return, and (3) there are no initial or ongoing fees or commissions.

While you own an annuity, you are free to make withdrawals. You do not have to give a reason why part or all of the interest or principal is needed. Withdrawal requests must be in writing. By law, most companies must send you a check within seven days. Often, a check can be sent out or funds wired even faster. Some companies let you make withdrawals several times a year; others restrict this privilege to one request per annum.

When you buy an annuity, you do not pay any commissions or fees. One hundred percent of your money goes to work for you immediately.

As you might have guessed, no investment is this good

without having some strings attached. The four disadvantages of fixed-rate annuities are: (1) the rate offered may not be competitive, (2) there is a fluke chance that your principal, and any accumulated growth or interest, could be tied up for a few years if the issuer runs into financial difficulties, (3) money taken out may be subject to a penalty, and (4) there is no guarantee that the renewal rate will be competitive.

Fixed-rate annuities also face the same risk that most of the investments shown in this chapter possess: purchasing power risk. Fortunately, their historic rates of return, coupled with faster growth due to tax-deferral (an important feature outside of a qualified retirement account), means that this investment has a much better chance of outpacing inflation than most of the more traditional, safe investments.

In general terms, the rate offered by fixed-rate annuities follows the prime interest rate up to a point. As you might imagine, contract rates have varied quite a bit over the past several decades. Since interest rates dropped steadily throughout most of the 1980s and early 1990s, this means that initial and renewal rates offered by annuities have also dropped by several percentage points.

For the most part, annuity rates have been higher than the rates offered by bank CDs in the past. There are no safer investments than those backed by the U.S. government, guaranteed by the government, or guaranteed by an insurance company. It is the historical and financial safety of the insurance industry that makes fixed-rate annuities such a safe bet.

Annuities are a clear choice for the investor who is looking for the utmost in safety and a competitive or better than average return (yield), and understands that because of the insurance company penalty, this is not an alternative to highly liquid investments such as money market accounts, T-bills, and CDs that mature in just a few months.

401(k) Considerations

A number of companies allow their employees to contribute 401(k) money only into an annuity. Fixed-rate annuities are not particularly exciting, but their return is guaranteed. If this is your only choice, you may still be able to select one or more different maturities. Since no one knows what interest rates will do next week, much less next quarter or next year, in the long run you will be better off opting for an annuity whose rate is guaranteed for a few years (similar to buying intermediate-term bonds).

If your company allows you to choose between a fixed and a variable annuity, chances are that you will fare better, or much better, in a variable annuity that allows you to select one or more different stock and bond subaccounts. Fixed-rate annuities are only for the very conservative.

Since money in all annuities grows and compounds tax-deferred, given the choice, you should use annuities for nonretirement accounts. There is no benefit to be gained by putting a shelter (annuities) inside a shelter (a qualified retirement plan). Since annuities are more costly to administer than mutual funds, you will, given the choice, fare better in a mutual fund.

ZERO-COUPON BONDS

Volatility	Moderate to very high
Total return potential	Fair to good
Recommended holding period	1-3 years

The U.S. government, municipalities, and corporations issue bonds to raise money. In return for borrowing your money, these entities promise to pay you a certain rate of return and the face amount of the bond upon its maturity.

Bonds come in many different maturities, ranging from just a couple of years to 30 years or more.

Zero-coupon bonds are a type of bond. They are distinguished from other types of bonds by the fact that they pay no interest, therefore there is no "coupon" (hence the name "zero-coupon"). Instead, the issuer promises simply to pay you the full face value when the instrument matures. The difference between your purchase price and the maturity value represents compounded interest. It is for this reason that zero-coupon bonds sell for less than face value, also known as par. The rate of return you receive depends upon the general level of interest rates and the maturity of the security. For the most part, the longer the maturity you are willing to accept, the greater the yield you will receive. At the time of purchase, your broker will be able to tell you the rate of return that you have locked in. If a zero-coupon bond is sold prior to maturity, the investor may receive a higher or lower yield than was quoted.

There are several advantages to zero-coupon bonds. First, you know exactly what you will end up with if you hold the bond to maturity. Second, the rate of return on the investment can be easily determined. Third, this is an easy investment to own. By this I mean that there is nothing for the investor to do; there are no interest payments that have to be reinvested—"interest payments" automatically go back into the bond. Fourth, you have a wide range of returns, degrees of safety, and maturities from which to choose. Fifth, zero-coupon bonds can be sold at any time. Finally, they have the potential for appreciation.

Just like other investments, this one also has disadvantages: (1) There is no current income to reinvest in the event interest rates are increasing, (2) the issuer could default, and (3) a sale before maturity can result in a loss. Like other debt instruments, zero-coupon bonds are subject to purchasing power risk. A risk rarely talked about when it comes to bonds of all kinds, is the *call risk*. A great number of municipal and corporate bonds, including zeros, include a provision allowing the issuer to "call them away" from the investor at a certain price. What this means to the investor is that a corporation or municipality can force you to sell the bond back to them at a certain date.

The other risk of owning zeros is only found with municipal and corporate issues. This is the risk of default. When you buy one of these types of zeros, ask your adviser or broker what the rating is; normally, you should stay away from anything that is rated less than "investment grade."

Since their introduction in the early 1980s, zeros have performed extremely well. This is due to the fact that interest rates fell dramatically in the 1980s. As you may recall, the prime rate hit 21.5 percent briefly in 1981 and was less than 8 percent by the end of 1987. If regular bonds did so well, imagine how zeros, with their enhanced volatility, performed. Thus, for most years during the 1980s and early 1990s, zeros racked up total return figures that were quite impressive. Although no one can say for sure, it is doubtful that zero-coupon bonds will do nearly as well during the second half of the 1990s (since it is virtually impossible that rates will again fall by 5 to 7 percentage points).

Since the accreted interest is taxable (a 1099 is issued at the end of each year), corporate and government zeros should be included only as part of a qualified retirement plan such as a 401(k) or as part of a variable annuity. Interest from *municipal* bonds is generally exempt from taxes, and so this type of zero should be owned only *outside* of an annuity or retirement plan.

If zeros can be sheltered from current taxation, they are an attractive 401(k) choice for someone who wants a locked-in rate of return. It is this feature and the safety factor that make zeros a frequent selection for a child's college fund or for retirement.

Zeros can also be used by aggressive investors. If someone is betting that interest rates are going to fall by one or more percentage points, this person should buy long-term zero-coupon bonds. If rates do fall, the capital gains can be quite high (a two-percentage-point drop in long-term rates translates into a 32 to 48 percent profit). If rates go up instead of down, the loss is also quite high.

401(k) Considerations

Zero-coupon corporate and government bonds are best suited for qualified retirement accounts because the "phantom interest" generated each year is sheltered from current taxation. One of the two biggest *potential* disadvantages of owning zeros outside a qualified retirement account is that even though the investor does not receive interest (instead, interest is accreted, or credited, to the bond), he or she is still taxed on it.

The other potential disadvantage of zeros has to do with volatility. Since these bonds can fluctuate wildly in value, they should be part of your 401(k) only if you believe interest rates have peaked (if rates then start to decline, the capital gains from a zero can be quite high) or if you are patient and willing to own this investment until it matures.

There is a good chance that you will *not* be offered zeros as an option within your 401(k) plan. Since most plans are limited to insurance or mutual fund products, you will not have the option of buying these securities on your own. Only a handful of mutual fund and insurance companies have zero-coupon bond portfolios. However, you can still end up owning zeros if you have your own IRA or if you invest non-qualified retirement money in a variable annuity.

Conceptually, you should probably avoid zeros unless interest rates are at some kind of historic high. Zero-coupon bonds are a very popular investment, but part of this popularity is due to investor ignorance.

HIGH-YIELD CORPORATE BOND FUNDS

Volatility	Low to moderate
Total return potential	Good
Recommended holding period	3-10 years

Close to 90 percent of all corporations would be forced to issue high-yield, or "junk," bonds if they issued debt instruments. Junk bonds are less-than-investment grade. These are securities with a rating lower than Baa (Moody's) or BBB (Standard & Poor's).

Bonds are issued by corporations in order to raise money. If the issuing corporations were more financially secure and/or had been around longer, they would issue investment-grade, also known as "bank quality," bonds. Since the great majority of corporations in America do not have the financial clout to issue AAA-, AA-, A- or Baa-rated bonds, they are forced to issue "junk." Investors are attracted to high-yield bonds because of their better-than-average rate of return.

In reality, there is a big difference between junk and high-yield bonds, even though these terms are frequently used to mean the same thing. *Junk* bonds are debt instruments that were used for corporate takeovers. *High-yield* bonds are securities that have had a long track record of overall reliability for the timely payment of interest and principal; they also represent those bonds that have had comparatively few defaults.

High-yield corporate bond funds, within the context of this book, are simply mutual funds whose objective is a high current income while preserving principal. These funds are willing to sacrifice a little bit of the current income (accepting, say, 9 percent instead of 11 to 13 percent) in return for having bonds at the high end of the junk bond spectrum (e.g., B- or BB-rated bonds instead of CCC-, CC- or C-rated securities).

There are two advantages to high-yield bonds: (1) a better current return and (2) reduced volatility. As already mentioned, people who buy these securities expect something extra in return for taking on more financial risk. Financial risk refers to the possibility that the corporation may go into bankruptcy, foreclosure, or reorganization. As scary as this sounds, less than 1 percent of the corporate bonds outstanding experience such troubles each year. Equally important, corporations that have such problems often are able to turn themselves around and show a profit as well as pay off all bondholders.

The second advantage, reduced volatility, has already been described in other sections. Briefly, lower fluctuations in value are beneficial to an investor who may want to sell his or her bonds prior to their maturity. If your underlying principal does not go up or down very much in value, there is a greater chance that you will be made whole at the time of sale. Volatility, however, is a two-way street. When interest rates are falling and bond prices are going up, you will wish that you owned more volatile bonds. It is only when rates are *increasing* that you want to own more stable securities.

With high-yield bond funds, you also get the advantage of ongoing, professional management, reduced risk, and the ability to switch among other funds within the same family with a simple phone call. The price per share (value) of high-yield bond funds is reported in the mutual fund section of the newspaper each day.

There are two disadvantages to high-yield bonds: (1) credit, or financial, risk and (2) price changes during poor or uncertain economic periods. You may be surprised to learn that during most periods of time, junk bonds have outperformed high-quality corporate, municipal, and U.S. government securities. Their return has been better on a current yield, or return, basis and on a total return basis. Even for the past ten years ending 1993 or 1994, junk bonds had better returns. This, despite the beating that most junk bonds took during 1989 and 1990.

When measured by total return, there certainly have been periods of time when safer securities performed much better than their high-yield brethren. Yet, over most of these same time horizons, and particularly when you look at ten-year or longer periods of time, junk bonds are normally the winner when compared to other U.S. bonds.

To see how these bonds have fared over shorter periods of time, let us look at all of the five-year periods beginning with 1982 (the figures are based on information from two different high-yield bond indices). The figures that follow are total, not annualized, return numbers:

1982-1986	+121%
1983-1987	+75%
1984-1988	+69%
1985-1989	+59%
1986-1990	+17%
1987-1991	+41%
1988-1992	+62%
1989-1993	+71%
1990-1994	+66%
1991-1995	+115%

There are certainly high-yield bond funds that have fared better (and worse) than this index. As an investor, your goal should be to select a fund that has consistently rated in the top third of its field.

Since junk bonds throw off a substantial amount of current income, they are most effectively used, taxwise, in a qualified retirement plan or within a variable annuity. They are also appropriate for investors who are in a low tax bracket and may or may not be able to shelter such income.

High-yield bonds perform best and are certainly more stable if they are held for at least five years. Such a holding period will help amortize any future disasters such as were experienced in 1989 and 1990. However, it is very doubtful that these bonds will go through losses as severe as this in the future. Now that the marketplace has seen what can happen to junk bonds, it is likely to learn from its past excesses and weed out those issues that are based on rosy predictions.

401(k) Considerations

Since high-yield bonds are often referred to as a hybrid security (acting partly like a stock and partly like a bond), they are one of the best choices for someone who is not sure whether he or she wants to be in the stock or the bond market. A fair number of people are turned off by this investment because it pays a very high interest rate—interest that would be currently taxable unless it is part of a qualified retirement plan or within a variable insurance product.

The high-yield bond market has evolved quite a bit over the past several years. The overall excellent track record of these debt instruments makes them a better choice than other forms of bonds in almost all circumstances. The only time a government or high-quality corporate bond would be a better choice would be if the country was in a severe recession or depression or interest rates were falling.

Unfortunately, well over half of the mutual fund and vari-

able life product families do not offer this type of portfolio. If
you are given the choice, include these hybrids. They have fair
to good appreciation potential, pay a very attractive interest
rate, and are more defensive than stocks or zero-coupon
bonds.

FOREIGN BONDS

Volatility	Low to moderate
Total return potential	Fairly good to good
Recommended holding period	1-6 years

Foreign, also known as international, bonds are issued by
entities (corporations or governments) in countries outside of
the United States. As with their U.S. counterparts, investors
receive interest payments twice a year and the face value
(principal) upon maturity. The bond is guaranteed by the
issuing corporation or government.

When you buy a bond, you are buying several things. First,
you are buying a degree of safety. The quality of your investment depends upon the financial strength of the issuer. Outside
rating services can help you determine the security of the
instrument. Second, you are buying current income. Third,
bond ownership can mean possible appreciation of principal.

When you buy a foreign bond, you are also "buying"
another country's currency. This means that your income will
vary depending upon the currency's conversion rate to the
U.S. dollar. If the foreign currency is up 2 percent against the
dollar, your check will be 2 percent higher. If, during another
period of time, the currency has dropped 3 percent against the
dollar, your income will also drop 3 percent. The principal
value at redemption or sale will also be affected by currency
movements.

For example, if you bought a German government or corporate bond five years ago when it took, say, 4 deutsche marks to equal one U.S. dollar and it now takes only 3.6 marks, then your original $10,000 purchase is now worth $11,000. This is because the deutsche mark has increased in value by 10 percent against the U.S. dollar over these five years. When you own a German bond, you are also, in a sense, owning deutsche marks.

There are five advantages to owning foreign bonds. First, they provide a current stream of income. Second, when properly purchased, they are also very safe. Third, there is appreciation potential, either from a drop in interest rates (remember, when rates fall, bond prices go up) or from an increase in the country's currency value against the dollar. Fourth, portfolio risk is reduced because your holdings are now more broadly diversified. Finally, you have more buying opportunities by going overseas. There are more securities to choose from whether your criterion is maturity, quality, or yield.

There are two possible disadvantages to owning international bonds. First, with foreign corporate bonds, as with any other corporate bond, and with certain foreign government bonds, there is always the chance of default, resulting in the loss not only of interest, but of principal. This negative can be eliminated by buying foreign government bonds from stable countries. The second potential disadvantage has to do with currency fluctuations.

The track record of foreign bonds has been quite impressive over the past one, five, and ten years. Consider the results of the Salomon World Bond Index (made up of foreign and U.S. bonds with remaining maturities of at least five years) versus those of the Shearson Government/Corporate Bond Index (high-grade corporate bonds and government obligations):

Time Period	World Bond Index	U.S. Bond Index
One year	+6.7%	-3.5%
Five years	+11.5%	+7.7%
Ten years	+15.1%	+9.8%

Note: These are average annual compound rates of return for periods ending 12/31/94.

As you can see, foreign bonds have done better over every one of these time periods. In fact, the results would be even more impressive if a pure foreign bond index were used instead of a world bond index.

One of the real beauties of foreign bonds is that they often move in a different direction from U.S. stocks. The results for both investments over an extended period of time can be quite impressive. From 7/1/82 (a month or two before the great bull market of the 1980s began) through 6/30/92, a $50,000 investment in the Salomon World Bond Index would have grown to just under $200,000, whereas a similar investment in the S&P 500 would have grown to just over $270,000. Even though U.S. stocks performed better, they also experienced about 50 percent more risk than a global bond portfolio.

401(k) Considerations

If you like foreign or international bonds, you are almost certainly going to have to look somewhere other than your retirement plan. Few mutual fund families or variable insurance product groups offer this option; therefore, it is highly unlikely that your employer will even be given the choice of including foreign bonds as an option.

This does not mean that you should not own foreign bonds outside of your company retirement plan. They are a good choice for other sheltered moneys, such as IRA accounts, variable annuities, and variable life. They are a smart choice for the conservative to somewhat moderate investor who understands that the best returns are often found overseas.

You should now have a very good understanding of the most popular kinds of debt instruments. Government bonds have not been included, since high-quality corporate bonds have performance and risk characteristics that are virtually identical for the 401(k) investor.

The next chapter covers the most popular equity investments that are found inside 401(k) plans. And, as with this chapter, it is likely that you will be offered only a handful of the equity investments described in the coming chapter. But, rest assured that even a couple of different equity choices can provide you with the diversification you're looking for.

CHAPTER 9
Investing in Equity Instruments

As you may recall from an earlier chapter, an equity instrument represents any investment in which you have an ownership interest. As an example, when you buy a home and take out a mortgage, you are an equity owner and the bank (or other lender) owns a debt instrument (the mortgage you took out). No matter how much the property appreciates, the lender is entitled only to the outstanding loan balance plus any interest due. Equity instruments may or may not offer a current yield or income.

Some stocks pay a dividend, whereas others do not. A dividend-paying stock is not necessarily better or worse than one that does not pay a dividend. A high-dividend-paying stock *conceptually* has less risk than a stock that pays no dividend, since the owner of the dividend-paying stock has a certain amount of assurance that he or she will be getting some kind of yield during the year, whereas the owner of a stock that pays no dividend is relying on share price appreciation only. However, there certainly have been a number of cases of stocks that pay the equivalent of a 6 percent dividend, dropping 20 percent in value (for a net total return of -14 percent); as well as stocks that paid no dividend, appreciating in price by 25 percent during the year.

There are a great number of equity instruments that you can invest in; however, when it comes to 401(k) plans, the number is usually limited. Still, the options available under most plans are extensive enough for the great majority of employees. This chapter covers four of the most common investment choices available within a 401(k) plan. Those investment options are common stocks, utility stocks (a type of common stock), variable annuities, and foreign stocks.

As a participant in a 401(k) plan, it is very likely that you will be offered a few of these equity instruments in the form of a mutual fund or variable annuity. So, instead of being able to buy Apple Computer stock, for example, you would invest in the XYZ Growth Fund or the ABC Growth Variable Annuity Subaccount, which includes a number of different stocks. The portfolio offered to you may not include Apple, IBM, or whatever your favorite stock might be, but it will include a great number of stocks (equities) that will go up and down in value just like your favorite stocks.

The advantage of going into a portfolio (a mutual fund or variable annuity subaccount or variable life insurance account) is that you have instant diversification. You no longer have to worry about whether Apple, General Electric, or any other company will go bankrupt or suffer due to negative financial news. Instead, you will own part of a portfolio that might own seventy-five to three hundred different stocks. This is a much safer way to own the kinds of investments you like, without sacrificing performance. Furthermore, the actual buying and selling of these securities can be less expensive, meaning that your net return can end up being higher. Finally, when "packaged products" such as mutual funds and variable annuities are used, the costs to your employer are lower, making it more likely that your boss will continue to offer a 401(k) or other retirement plan.

You may have an investment option that includes the words "small cap" or "aggressive growth." Both of these phrases describe a portfolio of stocks that is more volatile than "growth." The return potential (and the loss potential) on a small-cap or aggressive growth mutual fund or variable annuity subaccount is generally much higher than that on common stocks or a growth fund. Again, your decision to include or stay away from such an investment should depend upon your time horizon, your tolerance for risk, and the composition of the balance of your portfolio. Even a conservative investor should consider a small-cap growth fund if he or she has little other exposure to equities.

Variable annuities, one of the investments described in this chapter, are not equities or even a specific investment. Instead, a variable annuity is like a mutual fund family, offering a number of investment options that can include a money market account, bond portfolio, and stocks. However, the best-performing portfolios inside a variable annuity are usually the equity accounts. Moreover, the costs of running a variable annuity (the overhead or administrative expenses) are almost always higher than those of a similar mutual fund family. Such additional costs, which subtract about another 1 percent per year from your gross returns, become a big deal when you are looking at a money market account or bond account that may average only 4 to 7 percent a year. These expenses, which, by the way, are somewhat or fully offset by the additional benefits provided by annuities (and are fully described below) are much less intrusive when you are in a stock account that is making 10 to 15 percent a year.

Each of the discussions of the four investments examined below begins with a table that summarizes the volatility, total return potential, and recommended holding period. This table offers some general parameters and certainly does not encompass extraordinary events that could make this a better or worse investment. If you did not read the introductory pages to the previous chapter you should review them now to get a better understanding of what these terms mean and how they should be interpreted.

COMMON STOCKS

Volatility	Moderate to fairly high
Total return potential	Very good to excellent
Recommended holding period	3 to 30 years

Common stocks represent an ownership interest in a corporation. You cannot buy shares of a company unless someone is willing to sell them to you. Similarly, once you own shares, they can be sold only if there is a buyer. In the case of most stocks you would be considering, there is an active market and shares are traded by the thousands or millions Monday through Friday. Where the shares are traded depends on where the stock is listed. The biggest stock exchange is the New York Stock Exchange (NYSE), which accounts for about 75 percent of all exchange activity. The American Stock Exchange (AMEX) accounts for close to a fifth of the activity, and the remaining regional exchanges, located in places like San Francisco and Boston, account for the balance. Several thousand stocks are not traded on a formal exchange but instead are bought and sold "over-the-counter" (through a network of market makers). Part of this OTC market involving actively traded stocks is largely computerized through a sophisticated network known as NASDAQ.

A corporation has two ways to raise money: (1) by borrowing or (2) by selling people an interest or partial ownership in the business. Corporations borrow money from financial institutions or by issuing bonds. Ownership interests are sold by issuing stock.

If the existing owners of a corporation decide to "go public," this means that they are willing to sell part of the business in return for cash. The sale is made to the public via underwriters and investment bankers who help structure the stock offering (determine the price per share, the number of shares to be issued, what brokerage firms will be involved in the sale of the securities, etc.). A corporation that has already issued shares in the past is considered to be a public company since part, most, or all of the ownership is now in the hands of outside shareholders. A business that has already gone public can usually issue additional shares of stock to raise more capital.

There are two advantages to owning common stocks: (1) appreciation potential and (2) dividend income. Most people buy stocks for growth; they hope that they can buy shares for X dollars per share and later sell these same shares for X + Y. Historically, stocks have been the best hedge against inflation.

A large number of stocks also pay dividends. When a publicly traded corporation makes a profit it can either pay out part or most of that profit in the form of a dividend to its shareholders or retain the money for internal growth (i.e., more advertising, increased production, greater research and development, to buy other businesses, etc.).

There are three disadvantages to owning common stocks: (1) Some or all of your principal can be eroded if the price per share declines, (2) there is no guarantee that a company will pay a dividend, maintain its current dividend, or later increase its dividend, and (3) the decision to buy or sell can be "irrational."

When poeple buy stock, they do so because they feel the price per share will go up. They don't consider the chance that they'll lose money. Hundreds of millions of dollars are made and lost each day in the stock market. Fortunately, if a stock drops in price, the loss is only a "paper loss" until the shares are actually sold. Similarly, if the price per share rises from what you paid, the profit is also only on paper. You do not actually make or lose any money as a result of price increases or decreases until you sell some or all of your shares.

Owning stocks can be an emotional decision. It appeals to our instincts of fear and greed. People like to buy stocks when prices are going up and often sell when things look gloomy. Rationally, it is obvious that shares should be bought when prices are down (we like to buy other things on sale, so why not stocks?) and sold when a moderate or large profit has been made.

As a whole, the track record for common stocks has been excellent. This investment has outperformed real estate, bonds, bank CDs, art, rare coins, oil, gold, and any other investment you can think of. Long-term, common stocks have been the best-performing investment category, and the future looks even brighter than the past. This is not true with most other investments. Think about it. Gold is trading at half its early 1980s high; silver is trading at less than one-tenth its high; real estate prices are not likely to see their pre-1989 highs for several years (many areas of the country have had depressed real estate prices for over a decade); bond and CD yields are a fraction of what they were ten years ago; art, oil, and rare coin prices have collapsed. Yet stock prices continue to increase (as do corporate profits and scales of efficiency).

You can do well in the stock market by following two simple rules: (1) diversify and (2) be patient. No matter what someone tells you, no matter how convincing the writer or speaker, no one knows what the stock market will do tomorrow, next month, or next year. Predicting how an individual stock will perform is even more difficult (requiring great doses of luck). We do know that the stock market has always moved in an upward fashion and that the line of advancement is not always straight up. Often, stock prices "stray" and move sideways or even drop. Yet the market always recovers and goes on to make new highs. Sometimes it takes a week, a year, or five years for that new high to be reached. This is why patience is important. By diversifying and owning shares of several different stocks instead of just one or two, you will decrease your risk significantly.

To show the benefits of being patient and diversifying, consider the following two studies. If you had invested in the stock market for *one* year at any time during the past half century, your chances of making money would have been over 70 percent. If, instead, your holding period was extended from one to three or five years, your chances of making money were over 95 percent. Over any given ten years in a row (1973-1982, 1946-1995, etc.), the chances of showing a profit were 100 percent.

Turning to diversification, if you invest in one stock rather than a diversified portfolio of ten stocks, your risk level is about five times greater without any significant increase in return. As you can see, this is a situation in which risk (lack of diversification) is not commensurate with return (little, if any, return potential is added with a one- or two-stock portfolio).

There are three ways to own common stocks: individually, within a mutual fund, or within a variable annuity. Virtually everyone should own common stocks. Most people should own common stocks within a mutual fund or a variable annuity.

Despite the historical record, the majority of people do not have the temperament to own individual stocks. They tend to buy when the stock is reaching all-time highs, and sell when the market is at a low (after a stock market crash or "correction"). In general, people buy stock out of greed and sell because of fear.

If you decide to own individual stocks, make sure your portfolio is diversified. No matter how good your company looks or how hot a particular industry appears, it is best that no stock represent no more than 10 percent of your holdings (5 percent is even better and safer) and that any given industry (auto stocks, computer companies, health care, etc.) not take up more than 20 percent of your assets (10 to 15 percent would be even wiser). These figures may seem restrictive, but consider for a moment how your life would change if the stock or the industry collapsed. Although such a terrible event might not affect your standard of living now, it could taint your views about owning common stock in the future—and that would be a big, and far-reaching, mistake.

No one can say with precision that 20 percent (the national average) or some other percentage of your net worth should be in common stocks or mutual funds that invest in stocks. The weighting should depend upon your risk level and time horizon. If your goals are long-term (e.g., retire comfortably in 15 to 20 years, send two kids to college in ten years, etc.), then your portfolio should be dominated by stocks (preferably through mutual funds so that emotional buy and sell decisions are minimized), even if you are a conservative investor. On the other hand, if your time frame is one or two years, stock ownership, in any form, should be minimal unless you are at least a fairly aggressive investor. The longer your holding period, the more likely it is that you will make money in common stocks.

How much money should be earmarked for stocks also depends on the type of stocks you are considering. Some stocks are considered conservative and comparatively safe, such as utility companies; other stocks are considered to be of moderate risk, such as General Motors; others are considered to be somewhat risky, such as Apple Computer; still others can be described only as a gamble (any start-up company).

As a broad generalization, the amount of your portfolio that should be in stocks should range from 25 percent (if you are retired and conservative) to 100 percent (if you are middle-aged, working, investing money every year, and at least slightly aggressive). An older individual or couple may not be able to make up a loss in the market, but they also cannot afford not to have some type of hedge against inflation. A person in the forties or early fifties who plans on retiring in fifteen or more years has time on his or her side.

In a sense, there are two risks to stocks: owning them and *not* owning them. We have all heard about the risks of owning stocks, but few people talk about the risk of not owning stock. This is a point referred to earlier in the chapter. You want to own stocks not because they are fun and exciting, but because the price of goods and services goes up each year and few, if any, investments are as good a hedge against inflation.

A distant, secondary risk of owning stocks has to do with dividends. A company that has a history of paying dividends, perhaps even increasing dividends over the years, will probably continue to do so, but you have no recourse if the board of directors decides to either suspend or cut down the dividend. Stock dividends are not like bond interest payments, which are guaranteed by the issuing corporation.

Common stocks represent the easiest way, and perhaps the only long-term sure way, to make money. It is also easy to lose money in stocks. There is no one forcing you to hold onto a stock after it has dropped in value or stopping you from loading up on a "sure thing." The power of greed and fear is almost unlimited. This is one of the few investments in this book where it is possible to see substantial percentage drops in value unless there is diversification and patience. On the positive side, common stocks are the only investment that has consistently been a winner.

401(k) Considerations

There are a few ways in which you may be able to participate in common stocks within a 401(k): (1) direct ownership, (2) mutual funds, (3) variable annuities, and (4) variable life insurance. Most companies use either mutual funds or annuities for their 401(k) plan. The advantage of having your retirement plan in common stocks is that this will most likely be the best-performing part of the portfolio, particularly if a comparison is made after five or more years. In fact, there is better than a 50-50 chance that a stock portfolio will do better than a bond or money market account after one year. The disadvantage is that common stocks are a good way to take advantage of the capital gains tax—something you lose inside a qualified retirement plan such as a 401(k).

In general, a moderate or very large percentage of your retirement plans should be in stocks. They have an excellent track record, and since most people cannot touch retirement accounts for a number of years, one of the greatest downfalls of stock investors—moving money around too quickly—is minimized. A case can be made against common stocks, just as a case can be made against any investment; however, one would be bucking a track record that has been unmatched for about two hundred years.

UTILITY STOCKS

Volatility	Low to fairly low
Total return potential	Fairly good to good
Recommended holding period	2-20 years

A utility stock represents partial ownership in a utility company, such as a water company, telephone company, or power plant. As a small owner of the corporation, you participate in the success or shortcomings of the business. If the utility is able to get a rate hike, increase its user base, or add services, shareholders normally benefit by receiving a larger dividend and/or seeing the value of the stock increase. Conversely, if the Public Utilities Commission (PUC) continues to deny requests for user costs or the utility company is unsuccessful in one of its ventures (e.g., constructing a nuclear power plant), the price per share of the stock may fall and the dividend may be cut.

Normally a utility company has a monopoly or near monopoly on the service in a particular geographical area. It is this "captive audience" that makes utility stocks so popular. This, and the fact that people are likely to pay their utility bills—even before their income taxes—makes this investment unlike others.

Utility stocks offer several advantages. First, the trading range of most utility companies is fairly predictable; price changes are upward more often than downward. This means that no matter what price you pay per share, there is a good chance that when you go to sell your shares, you will see some moderate appreciation. Second, utilities offer some of the highest dividends when compared to other common stocks. This is because the majority of the profits are paid out to shareholders instead of being plowed back into the company for expansion or research purposes. Third, these types of stocks are quite popular. People like owning utility stocks because they are almost like owning a security that is part bond (the high current yield) and part stock (appreciation potential). In fact, utility stocks, preferred stocks, and convertibles are the closest things to bonds. Finally, unlike most other industry groups, utilities rarely face competition.

Next to the cost of fuel or power, the biggest expense incurred by a utilities company is normally the cost of debt. Utility companies typically have a great deal of outstanding loans that must be serviced. The interest paid on these bonds has a major impact on the company's net profits. Furthermore, utility companies are known for paying a high stock dividend; therefore, a great deal of money is sent out quarterly or semiannually to shareholders and bondholders. Thus, the general level of interest rates has a tremendous impact on this industry.

As interest rates fall, utility companies are often able to refinance portions of their total debt at much lower levels. By paying out less in interest, they have more money available for shareholders or for corporate reinvestment. Conversely, when interest rates are high, utility profits are squeezed. This type of environment can depress the stock's price and may cause the company to lower its dividend. As mentioned above, utility stocks are somewhat like bonds. And, like bonds, they are quite sensitive to changes in interest rates.

Although utility stocks as a group may have relatively low risk, you need to understand that risks in individual stocks can still be high. Companies with inefficient operations, mismanaged construction projects, hostile regulatory commissions, economically depressed service areas, or botched diversification schemes can and do have problems. Investors should not assume that a monopoly on the local power or gas business assures steady profits. Of the ninety-seven electric utility companies followed by *Value Line Survey* (a well-respected stock advisory service), twenty-three, or nearly one in four, have reduced or eliminated common stock dividends in the last six years.

For something that appears to be boring, utility stocks have fared quite well over the past five, ten, fifteen, and twenty years. In the past, anywhere from one-third to one-half of the total return from these securities (and mutual funds that specialize in utility stocks) has come from the dividend. Surprisingly, the balance has been due to share appreciation. The 1994 calendar year was particularly bad for this group; utility stocks as a whole suffered one of their worst years ever. Surprisingly, this makes them an even safer investment now (most, or all, of the downside risk has already been eliminated).

Keep in mind that utility companies do best when interest rates and the cost of fuel are low. Even though interest rates and fuel costs have varied widely, these ups and downs have still translated into a good, long-term track record for utilities. These stocks often outperform bonds but are considered to be not as safe when it comes to price stability. However, there have been periods of time when utility stocks have been less volatile than long-term government or high-quality corporate bonds.

Utilities can be an excellent addition to almost any portfolio. High-bracket taxpayers who do not currently own any utility stocks or mutual funds can reposition their retirement accounts or variable annuities to take advantage of this safe and reliable source of income and moderate growth. Low-bracket individuals and couples have more latitude.

Growth-oriented investors often shy away from utility issues, thinking that they do not possess enough appreciation potential. These people are not aware of the power of the dividend compounding year after year. There has been more than one ten- or fifteen-year period of time when the utility index has outperformed the S&P 500 and the Dow Jones Industrial Average.

401(k) Considerations

Utility stocks and mutual funds and variable life products that invest in these equities are a natural addition for
virtually any 401(k) plan participant. Utilities pay a very
high dividend (good for the very conservative investor), still
represent a monopolistic system that can perform well even
during a recession (people will pay their electric bills before
they pay Uncle Sam), and have decent price per share
appreciation potential (particularly after the first three quar-
ters of 1994, when a number of utility stocks were off 20 to
50 percent—the industry's worst performance in over twenty years).

A number of people ignore utilities because the dividend is
high and fully taxable. Within a retirement account, this
becomes a nonissue because of the sheltering. Still other people avoid utility stocks because they believe these securities to
be too conservative. A quick review of the industry's track
record would turn a number of these nonbelievers into utility
advocates. This investment category is recommended for most
401(k) plan participants—young and old alike, conservative
as well as moderate risk takers.

For purposes of added safety, most investors are better off
in utility *funds*, leaving specific security selection, analysis,
and ongoing monitoring to full-time professionals. Even an
investor who has the vast majority of his or her portfolio in
debt instruments (i.e., bonds, CDs, money market accounts,
etc.) should have a modest portion in utility stocks. Such an
investor would be better served by getting rid of some of the
debt instruments and buying into this conservative industry
group. In fact, the only type of investor who should probably
avoid utilities is the very aggressive person who is trying to
make a killing.

Utility stocks and utility mutual funds can be an excellent

alternative to fixed-income securities for current income and long-term protection from inflation.

VARIABLE ANNUITIES

Volatility	Low to high
Total return potential	Fair to excellent
Recommended holding period	1-30 years

A variable annuity is a lot like a mutual fund. The investor divides his or her money up among one or more portfolios within the "family of funds." Portfolios, known as *subaccounts*, range from conservative to aggressive. Most variable annuities offer at least the following investment options: money market, government bonds, growth stocks, growth and income stocks, and total return or balanced (a portfolio of stocks and bonds). A fair number of variable annuities also offer global stocks, foreign bonds, zero-coupon bonds, metals, high-yield corporate bonds, and a guaranteed fixed-rate account.

Just as in a mutual fund family, the investor is free to move money among the different subaccounts offered. Total return or yield is dependent upon how well the portfolio performs. Your investment choices, and risks, are limited only by the number of different funds offered by the variable annuity company.

Variable annuity subaccounts are professionally managed by individuals or teams. Many of these people also manage mutual funds that you may be familiar with; often, you can find a variable annuity that has a similar portfolio (in terms of risk, return, etc.) and the same manager as your favorite mutual fund.

There are four parties to every annuity contract: (1) the

contract owner, (2) the annuitant, (3) the beneficiary, and (4) the insurer. The *contract owner* is normally the investor. As the owner, you are free to add or take out money at any time. Just as with anything else you own, you are free to gift or will your interest to anyone you like. You can even substitute annuitants or beneficiaries at any time, without notifying them or getting their permission. In short, the contract owner calls all the shots.

The *annuitant* is similar to the insured in a life insurance policy. A variable annuity continues until either the owner says differently or the annuitant dies. When the annuitant dies, either tomorrow or decades from now, the contract may be terminated by the annuity company, depending upon contract provisions. The *beneficiary* is the person who receives the proceeds from the account(s). The *insurer* is the insurance company that issues the contract or policy.

The contract owner and the beneficiary can be one or more people. In fact, the contract owner and the beneficiary can be the same person or couple. Alternatively, the owner and/or beneficiary can be a living trust, child, parent, friend, or charity. The annuitant must be an individual; it cannot be a couple or a legal entity such as a trust.

What normally happens is that one spouse is the owner and annuitant (or there is a joint ownership, with each spouse owning half the contract) and the other spouse is the beneficiary. This way, if either spouse dies, the other is protected by either will, trust, or annuity contract. After the death of the first spouse, the survivor who inherits the account can change the beneficiary, perhaps naming one or more children as heirs.

There are nine advantages to variable annuities: (1) comparatively more consistent performance, (2) professional management, (3) a variety of investment options, (4) administrative and bookkeeping benefits, (5) tax deferral (a benefit for nonqualified money), (6) accountability, (7) probate avoidance, (8) no fees or commissions charged (however, most variable annuity contracts have an annual maintenance charge of approximately $35), and (9) a guaranteed death benefit.

Generally, variable annuities have more consistent performance than their mutual fund counterparts because this type of investment is considered longer-term than a mutual fund. Additionally, the portfolio manager tends to be more fully invested—the need for cash reserves is not as great. No matter what the investment objective, variable annuities also tend to be a little more conservatively invested than their mutual fund counterparts.

The second advantage, shared equally by mutual funds, is professional management. Even though your money alone will not attract a top-quality manager, combined with those of thousands of other investors, your money adds up to several tens or hundreds of millions of dollars. For a portfolio worth, say, $300 million, the typical fee of 0.5 to 1.0 percent per year can hire some of the best money managers in the world at a modest cost to you.

A full-time money manager can devote all of his or her attention to the selection of securities for your subaccount(s). Unlike stockbrokers and financial planners, who are constantly dealing with administrative tasks, attending meetings, and handling client questions and problems, a money manager's sole responsibility is to turn in good results consistent with the risk level of the portfolio.

Third, just like a mutual fund family, variable annuities offer several different investment choices (described above). The variety of options may be greater than you think. As an example, when you invest with a mutual fund company

(Oppenheimer or Vanguard, for example) you are limited to the management style of that company. Yet, with many variable annuities, you have the choice of multiple companies. As an example, the XYZ Variable Annuity may offer the following choices: Fidelity Growth and Income, Oppenheimer Growth, Van Eck Metals, American Growth, and Henderson for international stocks. Thus, what some variable annuities try to do is to find what they consider to be the best money managers within each mutual fund company. Since no mutual fund company excels in every category, several firms are used in the hope of getting excellent performance across the board.

Fourth, just like mutual funds, variable annuities offer investors a number of benefits, such as (1) quarterly statements, (2) toll-free telephone numbers, (3) performance reports, (4) exchange privileges within the family of "funds," (5) systematic withdrawal plans, if monthly income is needed, and (6) the ability to add or take out money whenever you like. Unlike mutual funds, which may charge a $5 fee to move part or all of your money from one fund to another, variable annuities let you make changes for free. In fact, there is no direct charge for any of the benefits described above.

The fifth benefit of variable annuities is tax deferral. There are several considerations concerning this point, none of which should concern you unless you are thinking about using this kind of investment vehicle for moneys outside of your 401(k) or other retirement plans.

Sixth, there is the issue of accountability. Unfortunately, there is no way to track the performance of a stockbroker. He or she may have a terrible track record and you would never know it (unless you experienced it firsthand). Variable annuities, however, are different. You can find out how a particular subaccount has performed over any time period you want by using one of several neutral sources.

The seventh advantage is that variable annuities avoid probate, just like a qualified retirement plan such as your 401(k), since a beneficiary is named on the application (and can be changed at any time). When the annuitant dies, the beneficiary or beneficiaries automatically take over the account, no matter what a will or living trust might say. The contract takes precedence over any other legal document. If your estate is subject to probate, at least the annuity will quickly pass to its intended heirs and the value of your estate, for determining probate fees, will be reduced accordingly.

Eighth, in most cases there is no commission charged to the investor. When you send in a check for, say, $15,000, the entire $15,000 goes to work for you as soon as the annuity company receives the money. With 100 percent of your investment going to work for you, the account value will double faster.

Last, but not least, there is a guaranteed death benefit. Variable annuities are the only investment that offers this guarantee. Here is how it works: At the time of the annuitant's death, the beneficiary or beneficiaries, which could be you, your spouse, your children, a friend, a living trust, etc., is guaranteed to receive either the initial investment (plus any subsequent contributions by the investor) or the account value on the date of death, *whichever is greater*. The only adjustment that is made is for any previous withdrawals made by the investor. Let's see how this benefit works.

Let's assume that you invested $100,000 in a variable annuity and decided to take a big risk by putting all of the money into the aggressive stock portfolio. At the time of the investment, you were fully aware that the return on the sub-account could be wild, rising or dropping by large percentages each year. In fact, let us suppose your account history looked like this:

Initial investment (6/16/92)	$100,000
Value on 12/31/92	$120,000
Value on 12/31/93	$185,000
Value on 12/31/94	$250,000
Value on 12/31/95	$194,000
Value on 12/31/96	$103,000
Value on 12/31/97	$81,000
Value on 12/31/98	$47,000
Value on date of death (3/6/99)	$29,000

As you can see, the value on the date of the annuitant's death was $29,000. However, the beneficiary will receive $100,000. If, instead, the account was worth $780,000 on the date of death, the beneficiary would receive $780,000. However, if withdrawals had been made during the life of the contract that totaled, say, $14,000, the death benefit would be reduced by $14,000.

As you can see, variable annuities allow you to take a certain amount of risk, knowing that at least your loved ones will be protected if the stock or bond market collapses and you die (assuming that you are the annuitant). You will not find this guarantee when you invest in stocks, bonds, real estate, or mutual funds.

There are four disadvantages to variable annuities. First, there is no assurance that your investment or the subaccounts will appreciate. As with most other investments, there is a chance that you can lose money (unless you choose a money market or fixed-rate account). Second, if you take out more than 10 percent of the account's value each year, you may be subject to a penalty. With most contracts, this penalty disappears completely after the fifth, sixth, or seventh year. Thus, if your account is worth, say, $56,000 next year, and your account is not old enough to avoid the penalty, you would be able to take out $5,600 during the year without cost, fee, or penalty. Any amount *above* $5,600 would be subject to a charge. Third, there are possible IRS penalties.

Finally, variable annuities are a little more expensive to operate than mutual funds. Typically, a variable annuity will charge a flat $30 annual contract maintenance fee as well as management and administrative expenses that are about three-quarters of a percentage point higher than those of a similar mutual fund. Like a mutual fund's expenses, all of these charges are hidden and described only in the prospectus. (The $30 contract maintenance charge is typically deducted and shown on your statement for the fourth quarter.)

These disadvantages or charges are a small price to pay for all of the advantages variable annuities offer. A talented investment counselor can help you find an annuity that can provide you with returns consistent with your risk level as well as a company that minimizes its expenses and investor fees.

The first variable annuities were offered to schoolteachers during the 1950s. This same variable annuity is still offered today (although its results can be described only as fair). The investment instruments that variable annuities invest in— stocks, bonds, real estate, metals, and money market instruments—have been around for a long time.

Overall, the performance of variable annuities is similar to the performance of mutual funds over the past several decades: Most of them are average, some are terrible, and a modest number have done extremely well. As with a fund, the trick to variable annuities is to pick one that has a consistent track record, stable management, and a risk level you can live with. Over the past five to ten years, the performance of many of the more popular variable annuity subaccount categories (aggressive growth, growth, growth and income, international stock, and balanced) has been very similar to that of their mutual fund counterparts.

Outside of a qualified retirement account, variable annuities are the perfect investment vehicle for an individual or couple who are in a high tax bracket and who want to accumulate money tax deferred in an account for future use or to leave to loved ones. Compared to similarly performing mutual funds, variable annuities are also a preferred choice if the investor is close to or over 59 1/2 (to avoid the 10 percent IRS penalty) and the money is invested in stock-oriented subaccounts.

Tax deferral in a bond account will probably not equal *tax-free* returns from municipal bonds unless the annuity is held for at least fifteen years. Moderate- and high-income taxpayers who want bonds in their portfolio should still consider variable annuities, but invest in bonds outside of the variable annuity by buying individual municipal issues, tax-free bond funds, or municipal bond unit trusts.

401(k) Considerations

For the 401(k) plan participant, variable annuities make sense if the guaranteed death benefit is important. Because of the performance of the overwhelming majority of these accounts, the chances of this feature's ever being exercised is extremely unlikely. Still, a number of investors, inside and outside of retirement plans, feel more comfortable having a death benefit that guarantees their original principal plus any additional contributions. Some products even offer an additional 5 percent enhanced death benefit each year.

For sheltered money, such as a 401(k), mutual funds with objectives similar to those that variable annuities offer are a better way to go. It is highly unlikely that your retirement plan offers both annuities *and* mutual funds, but if it does, choose funds—their operating costs and fees are 1 to 2 percent less per year than those of their variable annuity peers. Over time, a 1 to 2 percent cost advantage can make a big difference.

If you are married, the guaranteed death benefit provided by variable annuities (but not by mutual funds) can be a big psychological plus, particularly for older workers or younger employees who are nervous about the ups and downs of the market. If your 401(k) plan choices are limited to annuities, you will most likely do better in a variable annuity than you will in a more conservative fixed-rate annuity. If you do invest in a variable annuity, try to stick to the one or more stock portfolios offered. High-yield bonds and convertible securities are two more good choices. Because of the ongoing expenses of variable annuities, try to shy away from the other bond portfolios as well as money market accounts. The *net* returns on these subaccounts are usually not competitive.

FOREIGN STOCKS

Volatility	Moderate to fairly high
Total return potential	Good to excellent
Recommended holding period	3-30 years

Foreign, also known as international, stocks are issued by corporations outside of the United States. Like their American counterparts, foreign stocks represent ownership in businesses. As a shareholder, you own a small percentage of the corporation; if the company does well, so can you.

There are four advantages to buying foreign stocks. First, international issues help an investor reduce his or her risk through diversification. U.S. and foreign stocks do not usually move up and down together. When your U.S. securities are moving sideways or downward, your foreign issues may be increasing in value. Second, many foreign stocks pay quarterly dividends; these dividends are passed on to the shareholders. Third, foreign stocks, like any other stock, may appreciate in value. The common stock you paid $25 a share for may be worth $30 or $60 a couple of months or years from now. Fourth, since international stocks are traded on foreign exchanges, U.S. dollars must first be converted to the "currency of the realm" before a purchase is made. When the stock is sold, the transaction takes place in deutsche marks, yen, francs, etc., which are then converted back into U.S. dollars. This currency exchange can mean extra profit for the investor.

There are two principal disadvantages to owning foreign stocks. First, there is no guarantee that the stock will go up in value. It is possible that the stock could drop in value by anywhere from 1 to 100 percent (although the latter is highly unlikely, some publicly traded U.S. and foreign stocks do fail, and their stock becomes worthless). However, it is more likely that the stock will go up by several hundred percentage points over the course of five to ten years. Second, you may find that the foreign stock went up in value but that you have actually lost money as a result of a strong U.S. dollar.

Surprisingly, during most years, foreign stocks outperform U.S. equities. In fact, if you were to list the five top-performing stock markets from around the world for the last fourteen years, you would have a grid of seventy slots (five times fourteen). You might be surprised to learn that you would see the name "United States" on that grid only three times. In 1982 we had the second-best-performing market, in 1991 we had the third-best-performing market, and in 1992 we also had the third-best-performing market.

Performance figures for the decade from 1984 through 1993 also point to the benefits of owning international stocks. For the ten years ending December 31, 1993, U.S. stock market returns ranked thirteenth in the world.

These figures do not mean that the United States is a bad place to invest. On the contrary, a diversified portfolio of U.S. stocks has been an excellent investment in the past and will probably perform even better in the future. Foreign stocks have done better only because these international issues represent companies and countries that are often not as mature or as large as their U.S. counterparts.

Almost everyone should own some foreign stocks. If 30 percent of your total holdings (IRA, pension plan through work, regular account, spousal accounts, etc.) are in common stocks, then up to 60 percent of such stocks should be foreign issues. Such a weighting would be appropriate for a somewhat aggressive investor. A moderate or conservative portfolio would tone that figure down. These figures would be adjusted upward or downward depending upon how much of your total holdings were devoted to common stocks.

The reason why even conservative investors should have at least modest exposure to foreign stocks is that such a holding actually reduces your overall risk level. Foreign stocks alone are about 5 to 10 percent riskier than U.S. stocks; however, a *global* stock portfolio (foreign and U.S. stocks combined) has up to 51 percent *less* risk than a pure U.S. stock portfolio. Other studies, which cover different time periods, indicate that the risk reduction is only in the 20 to 35 percent range. I would still recommend foreign stocks even if there were zero reduction in risk because there is a potential for greater returns overseas. Any risk reduction is merely icing on the cake.

401(k) Considerations

If you are lucky enough to have a retirement plan that offers foreign or international stocks, either individually or as a portfolio within a mutual fund group or variable insurance product (variable annuities or variable life insurance), make sure that you put some of your money into this investment.

Overseas securities are a great way to add diversification to a portfolio, something not enough people do. Equally important, the long-term track record of this category is very appealing. Often, U.S. investors are turned off to foreign stocks after they have had a bad year (e.g., Mexico during the end of 1994 and during the first several months of 1995). Do not be distracted by this kind of volatility or loss.

The long-term view for international stocks has always been excellent. It is the occasional outrageously good or bad year in one or two countries that makes investors uncertain about this category. It is fair to say that almost everyone should have a global portfolio, one that includes domestic as well as foreign securities. Over time, you will discover that such a broad-based portfolio actually has less risk than a portfolio made up of only domestic stocks and bonds, and the performance should be better. This is particularly true if you avoid "emerging markets" such as Mexico, South America, and China.

The chapter that follows completes this triad of investment chapters. It is not a lengthy chapter, since there are only a small number of investments that fall into the classification of "hybrid."

CHAPTER 10
Investing in Hybrids

There is also a relatively small, but important, category of investments that are neither fish nor fowl. These are investments that act somewhat like stocks and somewhat like bonds. These investments are usually referred to as hybrids. The universe of hybrid investments includes convertible securities (i.e., a convertible bond that can be converted into the same company's common stock), balanced funds and subaccounts (mutual funds and variable annuity subaccounts that include both stocks and bonds), and certain kinds of REITs (real estate investment trusts).

Only the last two of these will be covered here. The hybrid investment option most commonly found within a 401(k) is a balanced fund. REITs are a distant second in popularity, but are included in this book because such information may be helpful to you when constructing an overall portfolio (including both your retirement and nonretirement accounts).

Each of the discussions of these investments begins with a table that summarizes the volatility, total return potential, and recommended holding period. This table provides some general parameters and certainly does not encompass extraordinary events that could make this a better or worse investment. If you did not read the introductory pages to Chapter 8, you should review them now to get a better understanding of what these terms mean and how they should be interpreted.

BALANCED FUNDS

Volatility	Low to moderate
Total return potential	Good
Recommended holding period	2-20 years

A balanced fund is a type of mutual fund. Like other types of mutual funds, balanced funds offer professional management, instant diversification, a track record that can be reviewed over any desired period, and services not found with other types of investments (e.g., telephone exchange privileges, easy-to-understand statements, immediate liquidations, etc.). Unlike other types of mutual funds, balanced funds invest in both stocks *and* bonds.

How much the balanced fund's manager invests in stocks versus bonds depends upon the manager's assessment of the economy, the direction of interest rates, and stock market optimism (or pessimism). Normally, at least 30 percent of such a fund's assets are in bonds; some funds may end up investing the great majority of their assets in bonds and convertible securities for brief or extended periods of time.

Restrictions on how the money is invested are described in the fund's prospectus (a booklet you are given at, or prior to, the time you make the investment). In the case of balanced funds, the prospectus points out how much (or how little) the fund may invest in stocks and/or bonds. The greater the range, the more latitude the manager has; if the prospectus states that at least 30 percent of the fund's assets will always be in bonds, the manager must follow this guideline, no matter how strongly he or she may feel about the stock market.

There are four great advantages to owning a balanced fund. First, the chances that common stocks and bonds will both go down in value in the same year are slim (when one goes down, the other often goes up). In fact, over the past half century, there have been only a handful of years in which stocks and bonds both posted losses for the calendar year. Second, since such a fund's portfolio is so well diversified, you can invest your money in just a couple of different types of mutual funds (balanced being one of them). Your resulting risk level will be quite low. In a way, you are admitting that you do not know (or care) which will do better, stocks or bonds. Third, the track record of balanced funds is surprisingly good. Although they are never the number one performing category, they are often towards the top of the list. Equally important, they are never at the bottom of the list (which is what can happen to a pure stock or bond fund). Finally, if you ever get tired of this investment, you can always exchange it for something else (such as a money market fund or government securities fund) by phone or letter.

The reason why balanced funds are not more frequently used, or mentioned, is that they lack the "sex appeal" or excitement of a stock or aggressive growth fund, and they also lack the perceived safety of a government bond or money market fund. (I say "perceived" because of the interest-rate and/or inflation risk that accompanies these latter two types of funds.) The manager of a balanced fund never appears on the cover of *Money* magazine or as a featured expert in *Barron's* or *The Wall Street Journal*. In a sense, the people that run these funds are the unsung heroes of the investment world.

Financial advisers often gloss over, or fail to mention, the benefits of a balanced fund because it offers too simple a solution to the problem of diversification. This is not the kind of fund that you are going to boast to your friends about. During a stock market crash, such a fund will fall, but not nearly as much as an aggressive growth, small-cap growth, growth, or growth and income fund. Yet, it will fall more than a high-quality bond fund. When the stock market is skyrocketing, a balanced fund will also go up, but not at the same speed or to the same heights.

The track record of balanced funds over the past one, three, five, ten, fifteen, and twenty-five years has been quite good. This type of fund is a steady performer. There are certainly periods of time when bank CDs, government bonds, and money market funds perform better, but such occurrences are the exception, not the rule.

Approximately once every decade, balanced funds will normally have a negative total return for the year. As mentioned above, there have been about five years in the past fifty when stocks and bonds both posted negative returns for the same year. A loss can happen in a balanced fund when interest rates go up by at least a few points *and* the stock market declines. When both of these events occur, the interest from the bonds added to the stock dividends may not be enough to offset the erosion of principal.

The only other risk of investing in a balanced fund is selecting a poorly performing fund. The chance of selecting a bad balanced fund can be greatly reduced if you are willing to do a little homework. By seeking out funds that have had the same manager(s) for at least the past five years, have a good track record on a year-by-year basis (rather than having a lot of ups and downs compared to other balanced funds), and have operating costs that are in line with those of balanced funds in general, investors are likely to end up with a winner.

The performance of balanced funds cannot be described as "exceptional," unless returns are measured on a risk-adjusted return basis. Exceptional and exciting returns are reserved for one or more of the different equity categories of mutual funds, such as aggressive growth, small cap growth, growth, growth and income, and foreign stock. However, these are also the same categories that also sometimes have returns that are "disappointing" or "negative."

One or more balanced funds could easily comprise up to two-thirds of an investor's portfolio. In fact, the only thing a risk-conscious person would need to add would be some international funds and a short-term bond (income) fund.

Balanced funds are a nice fit with almost any portfolio. They are not wild enough for the aggressive investor, yet they are appropriate for at least a modest portion of even a dyed-in-the-wool conservative individual or couple. Since they offer a certain amount of safety plus a hedge against inflation, they are a welcome addition to the portfolios of both young and old.

401(k) Considerations

If you are bewildered by all of the choices you have and do not know what to choose, balanced funds, or balanced subaccounts in the case of variable annuities, are always a good choice. Since these portfolios include both stocks and bonds, it is hard to go wrong. The track record of this category has been better than that of money market accounts, bank CDs, T-bills, T-notes, T-bonds, and corporate bonds over most periods.

The nice thing about using a balanced fund inside of your 401(k) is that you should not experience much downside volatility. This investment almost always has an annual record that ranges from "pretty good" to "very good" (i.e., 7 to 14 percent a year). If balanced funds appeal to you, put them inside of your retirement plan in order to postpone paying taxes on the interest thrown off from the bonds.

This is a good, middle-of-the-road approach to investing. It requires little or no homework or knowledge. It is one of the better choices for a 401(k) account.

REITS

Volatility	Low to moderate
Total return potential	Fairly good to good
Recommended holding period	3-7 years

One of the first, and often one of the better, investments most of us make is our home. Over time, real estate has outpaced the cost of living in periods of both inflation and recession. Traditionally, there have been four ways to invest in real estate: (1) home ownership, (2) the purchase of an investment property such as an apartment building, (3) limited partnerships, and (4) real estate investment trusts (REITs).

A real estate investment trust (REIT) invests in a pool of mortgages and/or properties. After deductions for expenses and management fees, income from the real estate and/or mortgages passes directly through to the investors in the REIT. The REIT is run by a board of directors who are elected by the investors. Each year, the investors have the ability to hire or fire one or more of these representatives. Board members are responsible for hiring property managers, accountants, and other staff and employees necessary to carry out the REIT's business.

Some REITs are finite in duration, others are infinite. If a REIT is finite, the REIT organizers intend that all properties (or mortgages) in the REIT be sold (or the mortgages mature) within a set number of years, usually somewhere between eight and twelve. Proceeds from properties or mortgages sold are distributed to the investors; they are not plowed back into the REIT (unless a sale occurs during the first few years of the REIT's life).

Most REITs are infinite-life. This means that when there is a sale or a mortgage matures, the REIT organizers use the proceeds to buy similar types of mortgages and/or properties.

There are three kinds of REITs: mortgage, equity, and hybrid.

Mortgage-backed REITs own a pool of mortgages and usually provide a high level of current income with little or no appreciation potential; in theory, mortgage REITs are less speculative than equity REITs. The REIT does not own any property, but instead has loaned its money to someone else. The property owner makes mortgage payments each month to the REIT. Each loan is secured by the property.

Mortgage REITs provide investors with a safe income stream from a number of mortgages. By owning a small part of several mortgages, instead of buying one or two trust deeds (or taking back a mortgage on your home), you greatly reduce your risk. If one mortgage defaults, you are not wiped out. Mortgage REITs provide greater current income than equity or hybrid REITs but have no growth potential (unless interest rates decline).

Equity REITs own properties and have the dual goal of growth plus current income. Equity REITs typically specialize in a type of project or geographic region. Some REITs buy only strip shopping centers; others concentrate on nursing facilities; still others buy commercial or residential property in a specific state or region. Whatever type of real estate you want to include in your portfolio, chances are that there is at least one equity REIT that specializes in that area.

Equity REITs provide some current income, which normally ranges from 5-10 percent, depending on the type of REIT. Approximately half of an equity REIT's total return is from growth and the other half from current distributions. Most equity REITs have built-in price increases in their income stream. Leases of the buildings have consumer price index (CPI) or overage (the REIT gets a certain percentage of gross sales) clauses built into the lease or rental agreements. This protects REIT investors against the effects of inflation. Some mortgage-backed REITs have equity participation clauses (the REIT investors get a certain percentage, usually 10-25 percent, of the appreciation of the property that is being used as collateral). Historically, equity REITs have dramatically outperformed mortgage-backed as well as hybrid REITs.

Hybrid REITs are a combination of a mortgage and an equity real estate investment trust. They invest in real estate and also purchase mortgages or make loans.

During the past few years, another form of real estate investing has begun to receive quite a bit of attention—a *mutual fund* that invests in REITs. A REIT can provide the investor with growth potential, income potential, and liquidity. Mutual funds that buy several different REITs provide all of these features plus geographic diversification, diversification of management, as well as diversification of different types of real estate.

REITs are a form of liquid real estate or mortgages. People own REIT shares for one of three reasons: current income, growth, or a combination of some growth and some income. They offer a way to participate in real estate without having to make a five- to ten-year commitment (or paying a series of real estate commissions, closing costs, and unexpected maintenance costs or having to deal with tenants). More important, REITs are an easy and cost-effective means of diversifying your real estate holdings geographically and by type. Imagine how long it would take you to become an expert in, say, commercial real estate in northern California or nursing homes in upstate New York—not to mention figuring out who would manage the property and how you would keep tabs on the managers.

The Wilshire Real Estate Securities Index is a market-capitalization weighted index which measures the performance of more than 85 securities. The companies in the Index are 79 percent equity and hybrid REITs and 21 percent real estate operating companies. From 1/1/80 through 12/31/94, a $10,000 investment in the Index grew to $40,422, while during the same period, the price of goods and services, as measured by the Consumer Price Index (CPI), almost doubled ($10,000 "grew" to $19,492).

However, not all REITs appreciate in value or are able to maintain their income distributions. As everyone who owns real estate (or acts as a lender) knows, property values do not go up every year; some years prices decline. Not every mortgage turns out to be a good one. Sometimes agreements have to be renegotiated so that the borrower does not go bankrupt. The fact that a mortgage REIT starts out with a 9 to 11 percent yield does not mean that the yield will not decline in the future.

Some REITs are more marketable than others. Just because a REIT is traded OTC or listed on the NYSE or AMEX does not mean that you will be able to sell your shares in a matter of a few minutes. Many REITs are thinly traded, meaning that there are comparatively few buyers and sellers. Your order to purchase or sell shares may stay unfilled for several minutes, hours, or days.

Before buying shares of a REIT, make sure that there are a good number of ongoing buyers and sellers. What you are looking for is trading activity. You want to make sure that when you decide to sell your shares, there are a number of buyers. Strong buyer interest means that you will get a fair market value for your shares. If, however, your REIT is thinly traded, the price you receive will almost certainly be less than what is fair.

Generally, REITs are interest-rate sensitive. When rates fall, mortgage REITs usually appreciate in value, just like long-term bonds. If interest rates fall and public confidence is relatively high, equity REITs usually also appreciate. Conversely, when interest rates are rising, a REIT may decline in value unless its income stream includes CPI adjustments.

The track record of REITs has been mixed. Historically, equity REITs have done quite well, often outperforming the stock and bond markets. Mortgage REITs have not performed nearly as well. Hybrid REITs fall somewhere in between.

As a result, equity REITs are a good addition to most portfolios. The idea of owning a diverse portfolio of real estate, with professional management and expertise, is quite appealing. The fact that you can buy into a REIT that owns a certain *type* of property or is active in a specific region is merely icing on the cake.

A similar case cannot be made for mortgage REITs. True, their income stream is much greater than that found in an equity or hybrid REIT, but there are better alternatives. When interest rates are low, good-quality high-yield bonds are a better choice—they are more marketable and have a better track record. When interest rates are high, bank CDs, government bonds, and tax-free municipal bonds often make better sense, particularly on a risk-adjusted basis.

401(k) Considerations

REITs are a mysterious investment to most people. This category does not get a lot of attention, despite its rather impressive long-term track record. Most years, this is not a very volatile investment; sporadically the industry can chalk up 20 to 30 percent gains or losses in a twelve-month period. Often more stable than stocks, particularly on a daily, weekly, or monthly basis, REITs are a good choice for most 401(k) participants.

REITs are a wise choice for retirement accounts because: (1) real estate is considered to be a long-term commitment, just like a 401(k), (2) the dividend stream, which can be quite high (ten percent with some companies), is sheltered, and (3) the properties are usually diversified either geographically or by type.

For purely income-oriented investors, there are usually better alternatives than REITs. However, for someone who is satisfied with a moderate level of income, coupled with deferred growth potential, this is a good way to go for up to 15 percent of your portfolio. Look for equity REITs that have been around for at least a decade and that have a history of meaningful dividend distributions and price appreciation. As with any other type of investment, do not expect the share price to increase every year. No type of real estate goes up each and every year.

This ends the three chapters that cover the investment choices you are likely to be offered inside your 401(k) plan. As you can see, the world of investing is not black and white. There are a number of advantages and disadvantages to *every* investment.

CHAPTER 11
Mutual Funds & Global Investing

This chapter has the same format as the previous three chapters.

Even though most of the discussion concerning investments in this book is generic in nature, the reality is that your 401(k) plan will probably not offer you the option of buying individual shares or bonds. Instead, you will most likely be offered choices within a mutual fund group or life insurance products.

Now that you have been well briefed about specific investments and the generic categories into which such investments fall, it is time to turn our attention to the advantages and disadvantages a mutual fund offers you, not only inside a 401(k), but as part of your overall investment strategy.

Along the same lines, global diversification has been discussed, but without much mention of any facts or performance figures. The second half of this chapter addresses these issues as well.

INDIVIDUAL SECURITIES VERSUS MUTUAL FUNDS

When you buy shares of a specific stock or a specific bond, you own an individual security. When you own shares of a mutual fund (or unit trust), you own a very small percentage of a pool of securities that includes many stocks and/or bonds.

Both types of investments are securities and as such are regulated by both state and federal agencies.

When you buy individual shares, you are betting on the fortunes of a specific company. If the company increases its profits or earnings, the stock often responds positively. If it becomes stronger financially, the rating—and usually the price—of its bonds may also go up. Conversely, if something goes wrong, the price of the corporation's securities may drop.

When you own shares of a mutual fund, you are not betting on how one, two, or even three companies will fare. Instead, you are placing your trust in a portfolio manager who has selected dozens and dozens of companies. The stocks or bonds in the portfolio may represent a specific industry but are more likely to represent a broad spectrum of different segments of the economy.

At the time you purchase a stock, you can request that the certificate remain at the brokerage firm (this is known as being held in "street name"), be sent to you (unless the purchase is made inside your retirement plan) or, in the case of mutual funds and unit trusts, be held by the issuing fund or unit trust group. In most cases, it is best to have the certificate held by the brokerage firm or the fund (unit trust) group. This makes any subsequent resale much easier. If certificates are held by the brokerage firm or mutual fund, dividends, capital gains, and/or interest payments can be automatically reinvested into additional shares of the fund. In the case of individual securities and unit trusts, any income or gain generated can go directly into a money market fund.

When you invest in individual securities, you face two types of risk: systematic and unsystematic. *Systematic* risk refers to the type of risk that cannot be diversified away in the stock or bond market. It represents market risk. Phrased another way, when the stock market takes a beating, a large number of stocks drop in value, even though their profits, market share, quality of management, or research have not changed. This type of risk represents 30 percent of the risk of investing in the stock or bond market.

Unsystematic risk represents the risk that is unique (for better or worse) to a particular corporation. These special features include management's abilities or style, market share, name recognition, market niche, the quality of research and development, or the use of a special formula, product, or service. This type of risk represents the other 70 percent of the "risk pie." It can be completely eliminated by diversification—by owning shares of just one mutual fund or by owning shares of twenty to thirty individual stocks or bonds.

What is surprising about the elimination of unsystematic risk is that it does not substantially decrease your potential returns. This is one of the few examples in the world of investing where risk is not commensurate with return. In fact, some studies show that there is no difference in return potential between a diversified portfolio and a one-, two-, or three-stock (or bond) portfolio.

However, there are risks involved in investing in mutual funds. The biggest risk is chasing last year's winner. The fact that an aggressive growth or biotech fund was up 68 percent last year does not mean that it cannot drop by 20 to 50 percent this year. There is virtually no relationship between a stock, bond, mutual fund, or unit trust's performance from one year to the next. In fact, there is a 50-50 chance that a top-performing fund will be in the bottom half next year, or the year after that.

The other risk of investing in mutual funds is not being properly diversified. Almost all investors are either too conservative (with their money stuck mostly in bond funds, CDs, and money market accounts) or too aggressive (going heavily

into specialty or aggressive growth funds). The key to successful investing is to strive for very good returns rather than
being content with CDs or, at the other end of the spectrum,
trying to double your money in just a couple of years.

Mutual funds offer many advantages. Funds provide professional, full-time management. It is not likely that you are
going to spend eight to ten hours a day following a portfolio of
stocks or bonds. They also offer you the ability to switch from
one portfolio to another for a small fee. If you exchanged several different stocks or bonds for different issues, the cost
would be several hundred dollars, even if you used a discount
brokerage firm. With a mutual fund, you can move your
investments from a growth fund to a government securities
fund by simply making a telephone call.

Mutual funds can be structured so that they pay you a
monthly income, no matter what type of funds you invest in;
a securities account at a brokerage firm cannot be set up this
way. Under what is known as a systematic withdrawal plan
(SWP), the fund sends the investor X dollars per month. Once
the account is set up for a SWP, you never have to make the
request again. Yet, if you want to terminate, suspend,
increase, or decrease the service, you can do so at any time,
without cost or fee. This one feature allows investors a steady
and predictable stream of monthly income, no matter what
the stock or bond market is doing.

Owning an individual security also has its advantages.
First, you can concentrate your investment in one company.
With some luck, the stock can increase in value dramatically.
Or, if a bond is not highly rated, the company's turnaround
can improve its rating, causing the bond to increase in value
considerably. Some investors like studying annual reports and
research papers on a specific corporation.

Owning individual stocks also has its disadvantages. No

matter how bright the future looks for a company, things change. Management quits, dies, or is replaced. Market share changes because of new products from competitors or an innovative advertising campaign. If earnings reports are disappointing, the price of the stock begins to slide. The fact that you have bought the stock or bond at its fifty-two-week low does not mean that it will not hit a new low tomorrow, next week, next month, or next year.

In the case of individual securities, the biggest risk is neglect, indecision, or just making bad decisions about when to buy or sell. Individual stocks and bonds are often sold based on a story or "pitch." A broker or adviser explains that you should buy stock X because the company is about to come out with a miracle cure or product. You may not understand that while breakthrough products or strategies may influence the price of a company's stock, there is often little relationship between the "sizzle" (the story) and the "steak" (the stock price). The fact is that stocks and bonds can go up or down in value, regardless of whether the product or breakthrough is successful.

Owning investments can be an emotional experience. People own investments out of fear (the safety of bank CDs and money market accounts), hope (to save enough to buy a house, pay for a college education, or retire), or greed (this thing is going to double in a couple of months). It is perhaps for some of these same reasons that most investors buy at market highs and sell at market lows.

When taken as a whole, the track record of mutual funds and unit trusts has been much better than that of individual securities. At first, this may strike you as odd; after all, mutual funds and unit trusts are made up of stocks and/or bonds. However, there are plenty of instances where a corporation has gone bankrupt and its investors have lost everything they've invested. There is not one example of a fund's going out of business and the shareholders losing all their money.

For most portfolios, individual securities are best suited as complements to other kinds of investments—such as highly-rated municipal or government bonds. Otherwise, you are probably better off owning different kinds of mutual funds to reach your desired level of diversification. A mutual fund or unit trust manager can watch over your portfolio full-time, with an objectivity that you probably don't possess. Equally important, the people running these portfolios often have a tremendous amount of experience and access to information that most individuals do not have the time or money to acquire. It can be extremely difficult to measure an investment's performance, or to devise a profitable strategy (e.g., do you buy more/sell out when the price drops/goes up 10 percent, 20 percent, 60 percent?). A mutual fund manager can remove most of this anxiety. A disciplined fund manager can look at the situation more objectively.

401(k) Considerations

The difference between individual securities and mutual funds (or other managed accounts such as variable life or variable annuities) is probably a moot point when it comes to your 401(k) or other retirement plan. In order to minimize costs and confusion, the great majority of employers opt for funds *or* insurance products. This may sound unfair, but it is not. Expensive retirement plans are paid for by the employees one way or another; there is a limit to the benefits an employer can provide.

If you like trading individual securities, you will find it easier and more rewarding outside of your retirement account. If you do participate in your company's 401(k) plan or other retirement account, your biggest concern should be that there are at least a handful of investment options for you to choose from. Being in the XYZ family of funds instead of the ABC group of funds will probably prove to be unimportant in the long run.

GLOBAL INVESTING

A global portfolio is one that invests in securities from several different countries, including the U.S. The securities can be stocks and/or bonds and may be issued by a country or by a corporation domiciled there. A *foreign* or international portfolio is one that invests exclusively outside of the United States. A domestic portfolio is composed solely of U.S. securities and assets.

You can take a domestic (United States only) portfolio and make it global very easily. Simply sell some of your U.S. securities and buy similar foreign securities. For example, if you own a government securities fund, you can exchange half of it for a foreign bond fund. If you have a growth fund, you can sell 30 to 50 percent of it and buy into a foreign equity fund. Alternatively, you could sell all of your individual stocks or bonds (or mutual funds and unit trusts) and use the money to buy a global stock and/or bond fund.

There are only two advantages to having a global portfolio: less risk and better returns. Sometimes a pure U.S. portfolio will have less risk than a foreign or global portfolio of similar securities, but this is the exception, not the rule. One of the major attractions of a global portfolio is its performance. The track record of both global stock and bond funds has been excellent over the years. While U.S. securities are lying flat or going down, the foreign part may be doing quite well. As an example, over the past twenty-five years, there have only been seven years when U.S. stocks were down. During each of these seven years, foreign stocks were either down by less or showed a positive return. Similarly, there have only been a few years when long-term U.S. government or corporate bonds showed a loss on a total return basis; during these same years, bonds in other countries were posting positive returns.

The table that follows shows the five best-performing major stock markets for each of the past ten years, ending 12/31/95.

The Five Best-Performing Stock Markets (1986-1995)

	First	Second	Third	Fourth	Fifth
	Switzerland	Sweden	United States	Spain	Netherlands
1995	+43%	+37%	+34%	+28%	+25%
	Finland	Norway	Japan	Sweden	Ireland
1994	+53%	+24%	+22%	+19%	+15%
	Hong Kong	Malaysia	Finland	New Zealand	Singapore
1993	+116%	+110%	+83%	+70%	+68%
	Hong Kong	Switzerland	United States	Singapore/ Malaysia	Netherlands
1992	+32%	+18%	+7%	+6%	+3%
	Hong Kong	Australia	United States	Singapore/ Malaysia	New Zealand
1991	+50%	+36%	+31%	+25%	+21%
	United Kingdom	Hong Kong	Austria	Norway	Denmark
1990	+10%	+9%	+7%	+1%	0
	Austria	Germany	Norway	Denmark	Singapore/ Malaysia
1989	+105%	+47%	+46%	+45%	+42%
	Belgium	Denmark	Sweden	Norway	France
1988	+55%	+54%	+49%	+43%	+39%
	Japan	Spain	United Kingdom	Canada	Denmark
1987	+43%	+38%	+35%	+15%	+14%
	Spain	Italy	Japan	Belgium	France
1986	+123%	+109%	+100%	+81%	+79%

The figures shown above are in U.S. dollars and therefore include those years when the dollar was strong as well as years when the dollar was weak compared to other currencies. These figures are from Morgan Stanley Capital International and include the reinvestment of dividends. Sometimes worldwide performance charts do not include the world's smaller stock markets. For example, in 1993 the world's best-performing market was Poland (+718%), followed by Turkey (+214%), and Zimbabwe (+123%).

There are two disadvantages to going global: psychology and currency. Most investors are afraid to own foreign stocks and/or bonds; these people feel that they do not know enough about such investments, and therefore, these investments must be riskier. The reality, however, is different. If you own shares of a growth fund or an individual stock or bond, say, IBM or GM, take out a piece of paper and pencil. Write down everything you know about that security. If you can write more than a small paragraph, congratulations are in order. Most people (and most brokers) are not as well informed.

The currency risk is the other potential disadvantage. I say "potential" because the value of the currencies of the different countries you have invested in can end up being a plus just as easily as a minus. When you own a foreign stock or bond, you hope the U.S. dollar declines against the currency of the issuing corporation. For example, if you own German bonds or stocks, you hope that the deutsche mark appreciates against the dollar while you own them. If, instead, the currency declines in value against the U.S. dollar, your profits will be lowered.

As an example, suppose the exchange rate is two Swiss francs to a dollar, and that your favorite Swiss stock (or bond) is selling for two francs. You would take your dollar, have the broker convert it into two francs, and buy one share of the

Swiss stock. If the stock went up in value to three francs, and the exchange rate was still two to one, your Swiss francs would be converted into $1.50, representing a 50 percent gain. Now, let's see what happens if the stock appreciates from a value of two to three francs, but that the dollar is now stronger—and it takes three francs (where it formerly took only two) to equal one dollar. In this second example, the 50 percent increase in the value of the stock is completely wiped out by the 50 percent decline in the franc's value. In this example, your net profit is zero.

The biggest risk of going global is choosing the "wrong" countries for your portfolio. These wrong choices are often nations whose stock markets have soared over the past few months or couple of years. Returns of 75 to 225 percent look very enticing; after all, who wouldn't want to double their money in just a few months? It's easy to forget that these same markets may decline by 20 to 80 percent during the next year.

A good example of this problem has been Mexico. During the early 1990s, the Mexican stock market soared. If your timing was just right, you made a killing. If it was wrong, you were almost wiped out. More to the point, the average annual return of the Mexican stock market over the past ten to fifteen years has been quite poor—something financial writers rarely write about.

By avoiding the "exciting" stock and bond markets, places where yields and returns are way out of line with those in the rest of the world, you greatly minimize the risks of being global. A good rule of thumb is to stay clear of what are referred to as "emerging markets"—stock markets that are not very old or that have done well recently but have done poorly for the last ten years. These are markets that would be described as erratic—places like Mexico, South America, and the former Eastern Bloc countries.

No portfolio should be without foreign securities. As of the middle of 1995, the total market capitalization of U.S. stocks topped $5 trillion, representing about 40 percent of the world's equity marketplace. Ultraconservative investors may want to add only foreign short-term government bonds and money market funds to their current U.S. holdings. Conservative investors should also consider some long-term foreign bonds and perhaps a risk-conscious international stock fund. Conservative to moderate investors should be more equally balanced between U.S. and foreign stocks, bonds, and money market accounts.

There are very few examples in the world of investing of getting a greater return with *less* risk. A global portfolio is one of these exceptions. If you have your portfolio spread out across several developed nations, only a small portion of your holdings will suffer if the U.S., Japanese, or some other market collapses.

A global portfolio also gives you the opportunity to be in places that appear more favorable than others. If a mutual fund manager sees that economic activity is picking up or interest rates are declining in one country, he or she can increase the fund's exposure to that particular market. Conversely, if it appears that a government is trying to choke off inflation or is doing something to depress business growth, security positions can be sold off and the proceeds used elsewhere. With a pure domestic portfolio, you do not have that type of flexibility.

401(k) Considerations

If your 401(k) includes the opportunity to invest in foreign securities (stocks and bonds), take it. A goal of every investor should be to have some consistency in his or her portfolio. U.S. stocks usually perform well and domestic bonds have decent returns, but not always; the same thing can be said for international equities and debt instruments. The probability that all four of these categories will turn in negative returns in the same year is about one in twenty. True, your overall return will rarely, if ever, be +18 percent for the year if you are this diversified, but if you're like most people, your sense of fear is much greater than your sense of greed. Be content with your portfolio's being a consistent winner—instead of sometimes being a star and sometimes being a bum.

As the U.S. economy becomes even more mature, a greater and greater percentage of our country's profits will come from overseas sales. By moving from a domestic to a global portfolio, you should experience not only greater returns but less volatility. During the 1980s, few mutual fund groups or insurance companies included a foreign securities account or fund of any kind. Today, you are lucky. A healthy percentage of both of these groups include at least one foreign or global portfolio. Virtually everyone should have somewhere between 10 and 50 percent of his or her holdings in international securities. Conservative investors will want to have a higher portion of this range in bonds, whereas those who range between somewhat conservative and fairly aggressive on the risk spectrum will look more exclusively to international stock funds or variable insurance subaccounts.

A global portfolio will increase your returns and increase the overall safety of your portfolio. And, when it gets right down to it, isn't that what we all want?

Two very important issues were examined in this chapter: (1) the benefits of diversification by using packaged products such as mutual funds (variable annuities work in a very similar fashion but usually include a guaranteed death benefit—a sort of mini-insurance policy), and (2) global diversification, a way of having your cake and eating it too—better returns with less risk.

The next chapter, "Life Insurance in Your 401(k)," covers the investment or risk transference options available to you as a plan participant. As you will see, life insurance can be a great thing to have, whether you are a conservative, moderate, or aggressive investor, provided you need such protection, provided the product is competitively priced, and provided the investment options or the guaranteed or historical rate of return compares favorably to that of other stand-alone investment options.

CHAPTER 12

Life Insurance in Your 401(k)

Insurance products have long offered investors not only peace of mind, but also some tremendous investments and tax benefits. However, in looking at insurance as part of a 401(k) plan, the advantages described in this chapter are not as important as the actual need for life coverage. In other words, if you do not need life insurance or a policy to supplement your existing coverage, skip this chapter.

WHO NEEDS LIFE INSURANCE?

The easiest way to determine whether you need life insurance is to ask the question, "If I were to die, would any of my loved ones be *financially* hurt?" If the answer to the question is no, then chances are good that you don't need coverage. Here are some situations in which life insurance is a good idea:

1. You own a home that has a mortgage that you help pay for.
2. You provide financial support to someone.
3. You are a homemaker who takes care of a loved one (e.g., children, a disabled parent, or aged grandparent).
4. You plan on providing financial support to someone during the next several years (e.g., a child is about to enter college or will be going to a private school, one of

your parents or in-laws is likely to need ongoing sup-
plemental income from you).

5. You wish to leave an estate to someone other than your
   spouse that has a net value (after paying off all debts,
   including any mortgages) in excess of $600,000.

6. You wish to leave an estate to someone other than your
   spouse that now has a net value of less than $600,000
   but that *could* become worth more than $600,000
   during the next one to ten years as a result of inflation,
   growth, or additional contributions.

7. You wish to leave an estate to your spouse, and you
   believe that the combined estate, upon your surviving
   spouse's death, will be worth in excess of $1.2 million,
   and you wish to protect the estate from estate taxes,
   meaning that you want your spouse's beneficiary (e.g.,
   a child or grandchildren) to inherit the entire estate,
   not the marginal amount left over after federal estate
   taxes have been taken out.

This list can be pared down even further depending upon
your current investment portfolio. That is, if your assets are
large enough to throw off enough income (or an orderly liqui-
dation would last long enough) to replace the financial support you are providing now or are expected to provide within
the next several years, life insurance *may* still not be necessary.

The word may is emphasized because of the issue of liquidity. Thus, depending upon the size of your estate, life
insurance is not necessary if your assets can be easily repositioned into investments that will provide the needed income
for loved ones. A few examples may help make this point.

Let's say that John and Mary Smith are married and have
a home with a large mortgage. Both work, and both contribute to the mortgage. Each hopes that if he or she dies, the

other will be able to stay in the house—something that would normally not be possible if either of their incomes ended. In this kind of situation, both spouses should have life insurance. However, if Mary has an investment portfolio with approximately the same value as the outstanding mortgage, there is no need to insure her *unless* the investments are tied up in something illiquid such as a closely held business, restricted or nonmarketable securities, or another piece of real estate.

For another example, let's say that Fred and Ethel Jones are married and have a combined estate of $2 million. The couple has decided that the survivor will inherit everything and that when the survivor dies, whatever is left will be divided evenly among the couple's three children. Fred and Ethel believe that it is perfectly acceptable if each child ends up netting only a couple of hundred thousand dollars apiece. Assume that Fred dies first, and that Ethel dies shortly thereafter, leaving a $2 million estate to the children. Since Fred left everything to Ethel upon his death, no estate taxes are due because of the unlimited marital deduction. However, upon Ethel's death, only $600,000 will be exempted from federal estate taxes. (The figure could have been $1,200,000 or more had Mr. and Mrs. Jones done some advance estate planning.) In this situation, approximately $1.4 million of the $2 million will be taxable. After paying federal estate taxes, about $900,000 will remain (plus the $600,000 that was excluded). This means that the three kids will still divide up $1.5 million.

Had Fred and Ethel purchased life insurance on either or both of their lives, the proceeds could have been used to offset part or all of the eventual estate tax liability. However, the cost of such insurance might have affected their standard of living. Some people might call Mr. and Mrs. Jones selfish because they were not willing to sacrifice the cost of life insurance in order to save the children several hundred thousand dollars in estate taxes. *Most* people would look at the situation and say that $1.5 million was still plenty.

Let's look at one more example. Sven Haynie is single and very successful financially. He has parents who plan on retiring in a few years. From what Sven knows of their style of living and current portfolio, it is obvious to him that he will probably need to supplement their income about $1,000 a month. Should Sven buy life insurance on himself, naming his parents as the beneficiaries? Not necessarily. Suppose Sven has a rental property that nets, after all expenses, $1,500 a month. Or, suppose Sven has an aggressive stock portfolio that is worth $300,000 but pays no dividends or income of any kind.

In either of the situations described above, Sven does not need life insurance. It is highly unlikely that Sven will predecease either parent. But, even if he does, he could leave the income property to his mom and dad. An income stream of $1,500, even reduced because of a bad economy or high vacancy factor, will offer the income supplement that Sven anticipated. The stock portfolio could be repositioned into interest-bearing securities such as government securities, high-yield bonds, utility stocks, or a growth and income fund that provided the desired monthly income.

True, the value of the aggressive stock portfolio, like the rental property, may be somewhat or substantially less than its current valuation at the point at which Sven dies, but either asset could also be worth much more. More to the point, each of these assets is valuable enough that an unexpected drop in value does not hurt their usefulness in supplementing Sven's parents' income.

There are a number of other cases that could be illustrated, but the necessary points have been made: (1) Current assets may offer a sufficient alternative to life insurance, and (2) there comes a point where you have to stop assuming "worst-case" circumstances in order to make intelligent plans.

One last point about estate liquidity: Do not let anyone convince you that stocks traded on the New York Stock Exchange, bank CDs, government securities, frequently traded municipal bonds, or any mutual fund cannot be easily liquidated. This is simply not true. Each of these items is as good as cash. It may take up to a week to get your hands on the proceeds from a sale, but the IRS is willing to wait up to nine months after a death for any estate taxes. Securities such as stocks, bonds, and mutual funds often fluctuate daily in price, but most people do not own highly-volatile investments.

For the purposes of our discussion, let's proceed on the assumption that you've determined that you still need life insurance.

THE ADVANTAGES OF LIFE INSURANCE WITHIN A 401(K)

There are a number of advantages to having life insurance as part of your qualified retirement plan. It offers: (1) a way of getting a deduction for part or all of the premiums being paid, (2) a conservative investment, part of which can become moderate or aggressive, (3) a certain degree of guarantee to both the employer and the employee, (4) a means of partially or fully avoiding certain IRS penalties, and (5) a reduction in administrative costs for the employer. Let's look at each of these five points in greater detail.

As you already know, employer contributions to your 401(k) are fully deductible by the employer and you do not have to report such contributions on your tax return. If you buy life insurance within a 401(k), the premiums paid are also deductible within certain limits. If the benefits end up being too great, you will be taxed on what the IRS considers to be the excess. However, the table used to determine the taxable portion of such contributions, known as "P.S. 58," downplays the real economic benefit of such "excesses"—meaning that if there is a tax due, it is usually a bargain compared to the value of the insurance you've bought.

In its traditional form, life insurance is a conservative investment. When the insured participant dies, the beneficiary or beneficiaries will receive a predetermined amount, regardless of how the stock or bond market is performing or the current financial condition of the employer or the state of the overall economy.

When whole life insurance is purchased, part of the premium payment goes to pay for insurance and part is earmarked for investment. With *traditional* whole life insurance, the portion that goes to the investment is conservatively invested, and the participant knows that the death benefit is guaranteed and that the investment portion is growing at a guaranteed rate. The rate of return often ends up being higher than the guaranteed rate, but regulations require that the minimum growth rate be shown.

With *universal* life insurance, a form of whole life, the portion of the premium that goes into investments is put in a money market-type account. This means that there will always be growth (you cannot lose money in this type of account), but the actual rate of return will depend upon the general level of interest rates. For example, in the very early 1980s, the rate of return on money market accounts was in the 10 to 15 percent range; by the early 1990s, the rate had fallen to below 5 percent. The advantage of universal life is that you know that your rate is competitive with that on other money market instruments. The disadvantage is that sometimes this rate may not be very appealing.

If the 401(k) is funded with *variable* life, another type of whole life insurance, the participant decides how the investment portion of the premium will be invested. Investment choices are limited by what the insurer offers. Some policies offer only a few choices, such as a stock or a bond portfolio. Other companies offer a wide array of investment options, ranging from the very conservative to the very aggressive. Investment selections can be changed during the year. The employee participates in the good and ill fortunes of the portfolio(s) chosen; yet, regardless of what happens, certain guarantees remain for both employer and employee.

The employer knows the costs of the insurance in advance. Depending on the coverage, these costs may be fixed. The employee knows that loved ones will be provided for, and what the minimum death benefit will be.

As discussed in Chapter 13, if you take too much out of your qualified retirement plan, the IRS will impose a 15 percent penalty tax, known as the excess accumulation tax (Internal Revenue Code section 4980A). However, if life insurance is part of the plan, it is not subject to the 15 percent penalty—to the extent that it is considered "pure insurance" and not an investment.

The final benefit of using life insurance in a 401(k) is reduced administrative costs. A 401(k) that includes only life insurance, known as a *fully insured plan*, is exempt from certain administrative requirements, meaning that compliance costs are lower. Additionally, some insurers aggressively market their services to the 401(k) marketplace and often offer employers savings in the form of lower setup cost and lower ongoing expenses.

THE DISADVANTAGES OF LIFE INSURANCE WITHIN A 401(K)

As with any investment or form of protection or risk transference, there are also potential disadvantages to including life insurance within a 401(k). These negatives can be eliminated by having the employer or investment adviser do some comparative shopping and become more educated about insurance companies and policy variations.

There are three possible negatives associated with using life insurance in a qualified retirement plan: (1) misuse, (2) non-competitive product selection, and (3) greater than expected administrative costs or penalties in general. Let's explore each of these three points in greater detail.

The issue of misuse was brought up at the beginning of the chapter. Using insurance as part of a 401(k) is a good idea only if you have not already fulfilled your life insurance needs.

Lack of competition can come in one of two forms. First, the amount you will pay for insurance can vary quite a bit from one insurer to another, just as bank CD rates can vary quite a bit. Obviously, you want to make sure you select a financially sound insurance company, but you also want to do some comparison shopping to find out how much will be paid for each $1,000 of coverage.

Second, any premium dollars that go into the investment side of the policy are going to be growing at a guaranteed or expected rate of return. Comparing guaranteed rates of return from one insurer to the next is not difficult, but anything more complex than this requires some skill. Suppose one company offers a variable product that includes a stock portfolio that has averaged 12 percent annually over the past five years and another insurer offers a similar portfolio that has averaged 10 percent over the same period. One cannot say offhand which is the better alternative because (1) the 10 percent portfolio may do much better over the next five years (there is little relationship between the performance of a stock or long-term bond portfolio from one period to the next, despite what fund ads might lead you to believe), (2) the stock portfolio that returned

10 percent may be made up of more conservative equities than the one that has averaged 12 percent, and (3) there may be a change in portfolio managers in either or both cases.

The final potential disadvantage of using life insurance as part of a 401(k) plan has to do with expenses. Some companies charge more than others to install or set up a plan. Some insurance contracts include penalties or provisions that may wipe out part or all of any cash built up in the early years of the policy. Some insurers price their product in such a way that they provide inexpensive insurance, but the investment part of the product is loaded with excessive fees. And some companies may offer a product that ends up being more attractive to younger employees than to older ones.

Fortunately, all of the potential disadvantages of life insurance in a 401(k) plan are just that, potential. Neutral advice from an insurance or investment adviser will greatly decrease your chances of making most *or any* of the possible poor choices described above.

GETTING INSURANCE COVERAGE

There are two ways for a company to offer insurance: (1) using group coverage that does not require a medical examination or (2) taking an insurance company-mandated exam. The latter approach provides less expensive overall coverage, since the insurer has a better idea of the potential risks involved.

Whatever form the employer chooses, the *amount* of coverage is usually based on what is contributed on behalf of each employee or his or her expected pension upon retirement. Thus, the 401(k) plan might state that each employee will receive a death benefit that is equal to his or her projected monthly retirement check multiplied by 90 (or any number less than 100).

If an exam is required for each plan participant, such results may not discriminate in favor of employees who are considered "highly compensated." If an employee does not pass the exam with flying colors, there are two alternatives. First, if the insurer is still willing to provide insurance for the additional risk, the employee can end up with less insurance. For example, most employees may end up with coverage that equals 80 times their expected monthly retirement benefit, while a few employees, who turn out to be substandard risks, end up with a death benefit equal to only 48 times their expected monthly retirement benefit.

IRS LIMITATIONS

The IRS allows life insurance to be part of certain qualified retirement plans such as 401(k)s, but only if it is "incidental," meaning that it represents less than a quarter of the total *cost* (as measured by adding together all contributions) of the plan. Because this measure is not always easy to determine, the IRS has come up with two tests. The first test is that the participant's insured death benefit cannot be greater than his or her expected monthly retirement benefit multiplied by 100. The second test is that the cumulative premiums paid on behalf of a participant must, at all times, be less than 50 percent of the plan contributions for that same participant if traditional whole life insurance is being used, or 25 percent if term or universal life insurance is being used.

Buying life insurance does not have to be complex or mysterious. By having insurance inside of your 401(k) plan, you are buying it with cheaper dollars (meaning pretax dollars) and perhaps with a little help from the boss (if the company is making any of the contribution).

CHAPTER 13
Distributions and Loans from Your 401(k) Plan

There will come a time when you, your heirs, or your loved ones will want to take money out of your 401(k) account. You may need the money to cope with an emergency, or simply need to buy something for your home, your kids, or yourself. You may need to take out funds because you've retired and need the money for expenses. Whatever the case, one of the great features of 401(k) plans is that there is more than one way to make a withdrawal. Whatever your need or desire, this chapter will show you how to get money out of your 401(k) account, no matter what your current age or situation.

Distributions and loans from your 401(k) are subject to a number of special rules and potential tax traps. Before you receive any money, you would be wise to consult an investment adviser for help in understanding these ramifications. Deciding which of your 401(k) sheltered investments to liquidate can make a big difference down the line.

Before requesting any money from your 401(k), find out what kind of distributions your plan allows. This information should be included in the summary plan description (SPD). Next, you'll have to decide whether the distribution should be taken in a lump sum or as a series of payments. There are income tax tradeoffs involved in this decision that should be considered in advance. If you decide on periodic payments, you will then have to determine a schedule based on your particular circumstances.

SPECIAL CIRCUMSTANCES

Under certain circumstances, money can be withdrawn from a 401(k) without penalty, even though the participant is under age 59 1/2. To qualify for such pre-59 1/2, penalty-free withdrawals, the money must be used to pay certain medical expenses, or be withdrawn by an employee who has become disabled. To qualify as a medical expense, the expense must be deductible by the taxpayer. This means that it, plus your other medical costs for the year, must exceed 7.5 percent of the adjusted gross income (AGI) shown on your 1040.

If you are under 59 1/2, your 401(k) may also allow you to make withdrawals (and not have to pay them back) for what are known as hardships. There are only a few situations that qualify as hardship: You need the money (1) to buy your first residence, (2) to avoid eviction or mortgage foreclosure, or (3) to pay for college tuition.

Hardship withdrawals are still subject to a 10 percent IRS penalty along with ordinary income taxes. Furthermore, you must show that you have no alternative sources of money. The amount taken out for hardship purposes cannot exceed the dollar figure required to meet the participant's immediate needs. A number of plans that allow hardship withdrawals forbid the participant from withdrawing anything other than the employee's tax-deductible contributions (i.e., not the earnings or growth on such contributions or any employer contributions or the earnings attributable to such employer contributions).

The 10 percent IRS penalty can be avoided in the following situations: (1) death, (2) disability, (3) retirement, or (4) termination of employment. Unlike a loan (described below), none of the withdrawals up to this point need to be paid back.

MINIMUM DISTRIBUTIONS ON RETIREMENT

Distributions from a 401(k) must begin no later than April 1 of the calendar year after the plan participant reaches age 70 1/2. The minimum initial distribution is calculated by taking the employee's account balance (as measured at the last valuation date prior to the year the participant reached 70 1/2) and dividing it by the participant's life expectancy, as determined by IRS tables. If the participant is married, a joint life expectancy table may be used instead. If the beneficiary is not the spouse of the participant, joint tables may still be used, but no provision or allowance is made for beneficiaries who are more than ten years younger than the participant. Payments can be further minimized by recalculating life expectancy each year. As an example, if your life expectancy were twenty years, nine years from now it would be more than eleven years.

If the minimum distribution is not made in time, or not enough money is taken out when required, the IRS imposes a 50 percent penalty on the shortfall (the difference between what should have been withdrawn and what was actually withdrawn). Furthermore, taxes are still due on the entire amount; there is no credit for any penalty paid.

As an example, let us suppose that it was determined that you should have taken $15,000 from your 401(k) this year. Instead, you withdrew $4,000. The IRS could impose a $5,500 penalty ($15,000 minus $4,000 multiplied by 50 percent) *and* tax you on the entire $15,000, even though you did not actually withdraw $15,000 and even though you already paid a $5,500 penalty. As you can see from this example, the IRS is very serious about your taking out at least the minimum each year.

IRA ROLLOVERS

One way to avoid immediate taxation or any penalty on a lump-sum distribution is to have your 401(k) account transferred through an IRA rollover (as distinguished from a regular IRA). If the rollover is "direct," meaning that the account is transferred from one institution to another and there is no "constructive receipt" by the participant or any other individual, no taxes or penalties will be imposed.

If a lump-sum check *is* made payable to an individual instead of an institutional IRA account during a rollover, the employer is required to withhold 20 percent of the proceeds. If this happens, the employee can still invest the remaining 80 percent in an IRA, but only if it is done within sixty days of receipt of the check. The 20 percent withheld can be recovered by the participant when he or she files his or her tax return for the year. In essence, the taxpayer is saying, "Look, IRS, you have already received X dollars from my employer as withholding. I now no longer owe you Y dollars for this tax year; instead, I owe you Y minus X—the 20 percent withheld by my former boss."

Rollovers are a great option in any of the following cases: (1) You have retired, but you do not want to make any taxable withdrawals just yet; (2) the company is terminating its qualified retirement plan, but you do not want to take out any money at this point; or (3) you want your account to continue to grow tax-deferred. Unfortunately, once the money is in an IRA, or even an IRA rollover account, five- and ten-year averaging is no longer an option. The possibility of a portion of such moneys being taxed at a capital gains rate also disappears. Furthermore, loans from an IRA or IRA rollover are not allowed.

Surprisingly, any distribution from a qualified plan such as a 401(k) is eligible for an IRA rollover unless it is a required minimum distribution (meaning that you are 70 1/2 or older), the payment is periodic and is expected to last for at least ten years, or it is a lifetime annuity.

There is one other negative to the IRA rollover; fortunately, it does not apply to most people. If the participant dies before withdrawing everything from the IRA rollover, the remaining balance is added to all other qualified retirement accounts that are now part of the estate. If all of these accounts, added together, exceed the greater of $150,000 or $144,551 (adjusted for inflation), the 15 percent penalty applies. Such a penalty is not reduced or eliminated even if the beneficiary is the surviving spouse or child.

Any amounts not rolled over within sixty days of receipt are subject to income taxes. On a more positive note, such distributions may be eligible for five- or ten-year averaging, and a portion may also be taxed at the generally more favorable capital gains rate of 20 percent.

The IRA rollover has been mentioned several times, but there are other types of rollovers that also avoid the tax penalty and income taxes. You can roll money from one qualified plan to another, similar plan, if the new plan permits such transfers. Thus, if Mary has a 401(k) plan with the Widget Company and decides to work for the ACME Corporation, which also has a 401(k) plan and permits transfers in, she can have her entire 401(k) account moved over to ACME.

LOANS FROM YOUR 401(K)

Since there is a 10 percent IRS penalty on most distributions made from a qualified retirement plan, plus income taxes due on the entire amount withdrawn, a tax-free loan, which avoids both of these negatives from your 401(k), can be a very appealing option. Although employees are legally allowed to

take out loans from a 401(k) and certain other types of qualified retirement plans, the plan document may not offer such a
provision. A loan provision increases the costs of administering
the plan. In order for you to even consider taking a loan, the
plan must specifically allow them. For purposes of this section,
let us assume that your 401(k) plan permits loans.

A loan provision, as described by Internal Revenue Code
section 4975(d), requires the following: (1) All participants
and their beneficiaries must be treated equally, (2) highly
compensated participants may not borrow more than others,
(3) any loans made must be in accordance with the written
provisions of the plan, (4) the borrower is charged a reasonable rate of interest (a little more or less than the then current
prime rate), and (5) all loans are properly secured (the participant's account balance is usually used as collateral).

Internal Revenue Code section 72(p) sets aggregate loan
limits; if these limits are not adhered to, the loan will be treated as a taxable distribution (and possibly incur the pre-59 1/2
10 percent IRS penalty). Outstanding loan balances to a participant or his or her beneficiary cannot exceed the lesser of
(1) $50,000 minus the highest outstanding loan balance dur-
ing the previous twelve months minus any outstanding balance on the date the new loan is made, or (2) one-half of the
employee's vested account balance. A loan of up to $10,000
can still be made, even if the total ends up being more than
one-half the participant's vested account balance, as long as it
fulfills the first condition (1).

Any loan made must be repaid within five years, unless the
proceeds are used to acquire a principal residence for the
employee or his or her surviving spouse. The interest paid on
any loan is paid back into the 401(k) for the benefit of the
borrower (you are, in essence, borrowing from yourself and
paying yourself back—with interest).

Interest on such loans is not deductible unless the loan is collateralized by a home mortgage. Even if a home mortgage is used to secure the loan, interest paid is not deductible if the borrower is a key employee or if the 401(k) plan is based on salary reductions (meaning the account was built up based on the employee's receiving less take-home pay with nothing extra coming out of the employer's pocket).

If the business is not incorporated, loans to an employer or anyone who owns more than 10 percent of the company are forbidden. If the business is an S corporation, any employee who owns more than 5 percent of the business is also forbidden to take out a loan.

SURVIVORSHIP ISSUES

Since a 401(k) is considered to be a type of profit-sharing plan, your spouse's consent to decisions concerning survivorship benefits is not required *if* your retirement account is payable as a death benefit to that spouse. If your beneficiary is *not* your surviving spouse, that spouse must be given the choice of selecting one of two death benefits: (1) a qualified preretirement survivor annuity or (2) a qualified joint and survivor annuity.

The *qualified preretirement survivor annuity* is an annuity for the life of the surviving spouse that must equal at least 50 percent of the employee's vested account balance as of the date of death. If no election is made, this type of annuity becomes automatic. However, if the 401(k) plan permits, the participant (employee) can opt for some other form of survivorship benefit, including no preretirement survivorship benefit at all or benefits payable to someone other than a spouse. No matter what option is selected, if potential spousal benefits are waived, the spouse must have consented to the waiver in writing. Such consent is usually part of the participant's application or enrollment package and is usually no more than a paragraph in length.

Prior to retiring, a 401(k) participant can change his or her survivorship election. Once an employee reaches age 35, he or she can opt out of the preretirement survivor annuity provided his spouse consents. This flexibility must be communicated by the employer to all vested participants who are at least 32 years old.

Choosing an option other than a preretirement survivor benefit as they get closer to retirement becomes more attractive for most participants. By doing so, the participant will receive a higher retirement check each month. (The one exception to this rule may be if the employer is subsidizing the retirement benefit—something that's not very likely.)

At first glance, it may appear foolish for the nonparticipating spouse to give up any kind of protection or benefit. However, with a comprehensive financial plan, you can develop an alternative course of action that is beneficial to both spouses while they are alive—and that still provides the survivor a larger monthly check than the 50 percent (or more) monthly check he or she would receive under the default plan. A simple example will illustrate this point.

Suppose John and Mary Smith are in the process of deciding what election they should make, assuming that they are looking for a lifetime annuity. The company's 401(k) plan states that if the survivorship benefit is chosen, the monthly check will drop from $1,000 to $600. This means that once John retires, John and Mary will receive $600 a month for as long as *either* spouse is alive. John, with Mary's permission, can opt for a $1,000 a month benefit, but that would mean that the couple will receive $1,000 a month until John's death and nothing thereafter. (John would continue to receive $1,000 a month after Mary's death, but not vice versa.)

Initially, it might look as if John was being too selfish—or Mary was being too short-sighted—in considering taking more money now ($1,000 versus $600 per month) but getting nothing once John dies. But let's look at another alternative. John can buy an insurance policy on his life for $200 a month, and the death benefit on this policy will give Mary $610 a month for the rest of her life. John and Mary would be wise to select the $1,000 a month option. Even after paying for the life insurance (Mary's protection in the future), the couple will have an extra $200 a month. And, equally important, if John predeceases Mary, she will receive $610 a month from the insurance company for the remainder of her life.

The *qualified joint and survivor annuity*, unlike the preretirement survivor annuity, comes into being once the participant retires. If your 401(k) includes a joint and survivor annuity, it is important for you to understand how it works.

Under a qualified joint and survivor annuity, the surviving spouse must be given a monthly benefit that ranges between 50 percent and 100 percent of the benefit that was provided while both spouses were alive. Furthermore, the benefit must continue even if the surviving spouse remarries. And, as previously mentioned, the nonparticipating spouse can elect not to receive this postretirement survivor benefit, but such election must be in writing.

A change of election (opting for another type of annuity or no annuity at all) can be made anytime up to ninety days after the "annuity starting date." The annuity starting date is that date on the calendar, sometime after the participant's retirement, when the first benefit is expected to be paid. It is the responsibility of the employer (and the plan administrator) to notify employees of the election period along with an explanation of the consequences of selecting a specific option.

Keep in mind that 401(k), defined-contribution, and profit-sharing plans do not have to meet the rules and requirements described above if (1) no annuity option is offered and (2) the employee's spouse is the beneficiary. If these annuity options are not offered, the employer can simplify the plan's administration and lower his or her costs.

PERIODIC VERSUS LUMP SUM DISTRIBUTIONS: WHICH IS BEST FOR YOU?

Usually, a 401(k) plan participant has the option of taking a lump-sum distribution or receiving a series of payments over time. If you elect a lump sum payment, the entire amount being distributed is subject to income taxes during the calendar year in which it is received. If the lump sum is rolled over into another qualified retirement plan, such as an IRA, no tax event is triggered. If the participant opts for periodic payments, he or she is taxed only on those distributions received during the calendar year. In any given situation, one alternative may be better than another as far as income taxes are concerned. However, there are other considerations.

The advantages of a lump-sum distribution are: (1) The distribution may be eligible for five- or ten-year averaging, and a portion may also be eligible for capital gains treatment, (2) proceeds can be invested as the participant sees fit, as he or she is no longer constrained by the investment choices within the 401(k) plan, and (3) the account balance can be rolled over into an IRA, possibly further postponing income taxes, allowing the participant a wider range of investment choices.

Periodic payments offer the following advantages: (1) The money is not taxed until it is received, (2) the tax shelter continues for whatever amount has not yet been distributed, and (3) the 401(k) plan may offer guarantees or investment choices that would be more costly or difficult to obtain elsewhere.

A periodic payment schedule may be better for you if (1) you are a conservative investor, and (2) based on your family history and health, your life expectancy is considered normal or greater than normal. A lump-sum distribution is often the better way to go if (1) you believe that you can get a higher return on the money somewhere else (e.g., an IRA rollover that is invested in high-yield bonds, stocks, or foreign securities), (2) because of the benefits of paying taxes at a more favorable rate, you will, overall, fare better with the after-tax lump-sum distribution than if you paid taxes on periodic distributions, or (3) you are not comfortable with the overall safety or investments offered by your existing 401(k) plan.

The reason that there is no clear-cut answer to the question of a lump-sum distribution versus periodic payments is that no one can predict the future. No one knows how long you are going to live, by how many years your spouse will survive you, or how certain investments such as common stocks or foreign bonds will perform. Nevertheless, by making reasonable assumptions (e.g., determining your tolerance for risk, looking at life expectancy tables, assuming that U.S. stocks will average about 12 percent and that foreign stocks should fare even better, etc.), you can make a more informed decision.

TAX CONSIDERATIONS

Whenever there is a partial or lump-sum distribution from a retirement plan such as a 401(k), state and federal income taxes need to be considered. Some state and local governments provide for a partial or complete exemption for qualified retirement plan distributions. Other states tax such distributions, but at a lower, more favorable rate. A number of states fully tax such distributions. And a few states take a more extreme position and tax your 401(k) distributions even if you have moved to another state or recently moved to their state.

Whatever state you live in, or move from after retirement, the tax concerns will always be much greater on the federal level. Let us focus on federal income taxes and see how different types of distributions are treated.

First, you will need to determine what portion of your total distributions were made with pretax (deductible) dollars. These include contributions made by your employer plus any contributions you made that were tax-deductible. Any and all contributions that were deductible have a zero cost basis. For the majority of 401(k) participants, 100 percent of the 401(k) will have a zero cost basis, meaning that everything that comes out is taxable.

Things become trickier if life insurance is involved. Some 401(k) plans allow participants to purchase life insurance. This enables an employee to buy a certain amount of life insurance and receive a *deduction* for the premium—something that would not be possible if the insurance policy was not part of a qualified retirement plan. Congress believes that buying up to a certain amount of life insurance with pretax dollars should be encouraged, but that anything above that amount should be taxable.

If life insurance is part of your 401(k) or other qualified retirement plan, figuring out what portion of the premiums paid has a zero cost basis is not difficult. You should be able to find the information you need on your tax returns. Any life insurance reported as taxable income on a participant's federal income tax return has a cost basis (meaning it was not originally deductible). These are what are known as "P.S. 58 costs" and can be more fully explained to you by your tax adviser. If you are, or were, self-employed, you have nothing to concern yourself with—P.S. 58 costs are not available for such individuals (meaning that all insurance premiums paid as part of a qualified retirement plan were fully taxable).

The 10 Percent IRS Penalty

Your primary concern should be avoiding the tax penalties imposed on early distributions. If you take money out of a 401(k) plan before reaching age 59 1/2, there is a 10 percent IRS penalty unless you meet one of the following conditions: (1) you are disabled, (2) you have significant medical expenses (as defined by Internal Revenue Code section 213), (3) you owe payment to a former spouse or dependent as specified in a qualified domestic relations order, (4) you've lost your job after age 55, or (5) your account will be paid out to you in a series of continuing payments, based on your life expectancy or the life expectancy of you and your spouse. Under condition (5), payments must continue for at least five years, even if you reach age 59 1/2 before the five years have elapsed.

Five-Year Income Averaging

Some qualified retirement plans, including 401(k)s, qualify for a special, one-time five-year income tax averaging that a participant may elect if all of the following conditions are met: (1) the distribution represents the entire value of the retirement account, (2) the entire distribution is made within the same calendar year, (3) the employee was in the plan for at least five years prior to the year of final distribution (if the distribution is due to the employee's death, the five-year requirement is waived), and (4) the distribution is due to the participant's reaching age 59 1/2 or older, employment having been terminated, or disability (this applies only to people who are self-employed).

If all of the aforementioned requirements are met, the participant may elect five-year income averaging. Such special treatment is not required or automatic, the participant must elect this computation on his or her tax return. Only one election is permitted per person. If the distribution is the result of the death of the participant, the beneficiary of the 401(k) may elect five-year averaging if the requirements in the paragraph above are met and if the deceased was at least age 59 1/2. Finally, five-year averaging is available to the spouse or former spouse of a participant who receives a total distribution of the plan as stated in a qualified domestic relations order (e.g., a divorce or separation) if the plan participant would have been eligible for such tax treatment.

There are four steps in determining the amount of tax due from a lump-sum distribution that qualifies for five-year averaging: (1) determine the *taxable* amount of the distribution, (2) subtract a "minimum distribution allowance" (see below), (3) divide the remaining figure by five, and (4) look up the tax due on this amount using the single taxpayer rate schedule but without any deductions or exclusions and multiply this figure by five.

As mentioned earlier, the taxable amount of the 401(k) will most likely be the value of the entire account. Still, you may wish to verify this and make sure that you made no after-tax contributions during your participation in the plan.

The minimum distribution allowance is the lesser of $10,000 or 50 percent of the lump sum reduced by 20 percent of the total taxable amount in excess of $20,000. If this sounds too confusing, it may help you to know that this second step can be eliminated altogether if the taxable amount of the plan distribution is $70,000 or more.

The third step is easy and is not affected by whether or not a minimum distribution allowance was taken. The remaining figure is divided by five. This "one-fifth" figure is the amount you will use in the fourth step—looking up the tax due, based on a single person's tax schedule (without any adjustments for credits or deductions). This tax figure is then multiplied by five.

Let us go through an example so that you better understand the four-step process. The following example uses 1994 tax rates (for a single person). The example will assume that the entire 401(k) account is taxable (meaning that all contributions were deductible by the employer and/or employee).

Step 1. Total value of the account = $50,000

Step 2. Calculate the minimum distribution allowance as the lesser of $10,000 or 1/2 of [$50,000 - 20% of $30,000 = $44,000]. The minimum distribution allowance is $10,000, since this figure is less than 1/2 of $44,000 (Note: $50,000 - $10,000 = $40,000).

Step 3. Take one-fifth of this figure. ($40,000/5 = $8,000)

Step 4. Determine the tax due on $8,000 and then multiply this figure by five.

If you elect five-year income averaging, IRS Form 4972 includes instructions and a detailed worksheet. The 401(k) plan administrator will report distributions on Form 1099-R.

Ten-Year Income Averaging

If you were age 50 before January 1, 1986 (i.e., if you were born before January 1, 1936), you can elect ten-year averaging instead. Again, this is an election, and, as with five-year averaging, the participant is not forced to calculate his or her taxes in this way. Ten-year averaging is used with 1986 tax rates (single, no exemptions or deductions) instead of current tax tables. The steps used are similar to those for five-year averaging, with "10" replacing "5" throughout the instructions (e.g., "one-tenth of" instead of "one-fifth of" and "multiply by ten" instead of "multiply by five"). Obviously, when possible, the participant will want to use ten-year averaging instead of five-year averaging if it results in a lower tax liability.

In general, five-year averaging will result in a lower tax than ten-year averaging if the lump-sum distribution is greater than $386,000. If your distribution is less than $386,000, chances are that you will be better off using ten-year averaging. The computations for both methods should still be made, since no one can predict what current tax tables will be when you are given the opportunity to make such an election.

Capital Gains Treatment

If you were born before January 1, 1936 and had participated in a 401(k) before 1974, you have one other possible election. The account balance *prior to 1974* can be taxed at a flat rate of 20 percent (the rate previously used for long-term capital gains). Like other elections or options, the capital gains computation is something that the participant would select only if the overall tax liability were lower than the amount due using the regular computation.

Capital gains treatment should be used whenever it is determined that the participant's 401(k) account value as of December 31, 1973 would otherwise be taxed at a rate greater than 20 percent. If this is the case, which it most likely would be, even with five- or ten-year averaging, a 20 percent tax rate is obviously better than a 21 percent or greater tax rate.

Death of the Participant

Up to $5,000 of what the beneficiary receives (referred to as the employee death benefit) may be excludable from income taxes. If a life insurance policy was part of the participant's 401(k), the portion of the policy that represents "pure insurance" is also excludable from income taxes. The pure insurance amount is the policy's face amount minus its cash value at the date of the participant's death. An example may also be helpful here.

John Doe, age 63, recently died, leaving his beneficiary $200,000 from a 401(k) plan. The entire $200,000 represents the proceeds of a life insurance policy that was purchased within the 401(k). On the date of John's death, the cash value of his policy was $120,000. During his lifetime, John had reported on his tax returns a cumulative total of $20,000 of P.S. 58 insurance costs. John's beneficiary will be taxed on $200,000 (face value) minus $120,000 (the cash value), or $80,000. This $80,000 can be further reduced by the $5,000 employee death benefit and by another $20,000 (the P.S. 58 costs that were not deductible by John). Thus, John's beneficiary will be taxed on $55,000, not $200,000.

John's beneficiary can elect five-year income averaging, and may be able to use ten-year averaging instead (if John was born before January 1, 1936). There is also the possibility that a portion of the $55,000 subject to taxation will be eligible for capital gains treatment (but only for pre-1974 amounts), again assuming that John was age 50 before January 1, 1986 and had a 401(k) account before 1974.

If a spouse is the beneficiary, he or she can elect to roll over the entire distribution into an IRA rollover and further postpone taxation. In such a situation, the surviving spouse would not be required to take any money out until he or she reaches age 70 1/2. In the example above, it is extremely doubtful that such an election would be made, since an IRA rollover would negate all of the reductions (from $200,000 down to $55,000) and would also eliminate the possibility of using five-year or ten-year averaging.

Estate Taxes

Whenever someone dies, there is always the possibility that their estate may be subject to taxes. Estate taxes affect only about 1 percent of all decedents' estates for two reasons. First, you may leave your spouse an unlimited dollar amount—none of it is subject to taxation upon your death. Second, you may also leave your child, children, relatives, or friends up to an additional $600,000 without triggering the estate tax.

As an example, suppose Mary dies and has an estate that was valued at $17,600,000 at her death. If Mary were married, she could leave $17,000,000 to her surviving spouse and $600,000 to her children. If Mary were to leave something less than $17,000,000 to her spouse, there would be an estate tax. (The $600,000 exclusion, which applies to heirs other than a spouse, is cumulative, not $600,000 per heir or beneficiary.)

Leaving a large estate to a spouse often merely postpones the taxable event. Eventually, the second spouse will die, and he or she will be able to leave only up to $600,000 free of federal estate taxes. Everyone has a $600,000 exclusion. You do not have to be married, have children, or even be an adult to get this exclusion—it is automatic. However, the *unlimited* marital deduction is available only to a married person. When the second spouse dies, estate taxes will be due on the net estate, once $600,000 is subtracted. The only way to further postpone such an event would be for the surviving spouse to remarry and leave everything in his or her estate to the new spouse.

Excess Distribution Penalties

As a way of generating more revenue, the IRS now imposes a penalty tax if you take too much money out of your 401(k), no matter what the circumstances (e.g., death, disability, reaching age 59 1/2, turning 70 1/2, etc.). The excess distribution penalty is 15 percent and applies to that part of any distributions that exceed $144,551 for the calendar year. The dollar figure is based on all distributions during the calendar year *from all qualified plans*, including, but not limited to, IRAs, Keoghs, and 401(k)s.

The dollar figures above are substantially higher if the plan recipient elects a lump-sum distribution. In such a case, the limit is increased fivefold: $722,755 (indexed for inflation) or $750,000, whichever is greater.

This chapter has included all of the information you need to make an informed decision as to when and how money can be taken out of your 401(k) account. The key to your financial success will mostly be determined by how disciplined you are in investing in the retirement plans being offered to you and deciding how your contributions are invested.

APPENDIX A
Commonly Asked Questions

Q: *What is the difference between a qualified and a nonqualified retirement plan?*

A 401(k) is a *qualified* retirement plan, meaning that contributions are tax-deductible. Some retirement plans are not qualified, meaning that all contributions are made with after-tax dollars (i.e., there is no tax deduction). Qualified plans are limited in terms of how much can be contributed, and deducted, each year, whereas nonqualified plans often have no dollar limits, since they do not provide any *immediate* tax benefit.

The advantage of using a nonqualified plan is that the employer can discriminate and decide who gets what benefits and how much. This means that certain key or favored employees can be included while others are excluded. In order to discourage such practices, the IRS, through legislation passed by Congress, does not allow such benefits to be tax-deductible and limits the types of investment vehicles (e.g., certain kinds of insurance products) that can be used if tax-deferred growth is desired.

Q: *What makes a 401(k) different from other retirement plans?*

A 401(k) plan provides more flexibility than most other kinds of qualified retirement plans. The plan can be set up so that contributions are made by the employer, the employee, or both. The employer can further encourage employees to contribute to their future well-being through a matching program (e.g., "For every dollar an employee puts in, the company will add an additional 25 cents"), which can translate into a great initial rate of return—25 percent in the example given in parentheses.

The ability to withdraw money for "hardship purposes" also makes a 401(k) plan different from its peers. Employees can take money out to purchase a home, send a child through school, or pay for medical care, all without penalty or cost. The money withdrawn must be repaid and interest must be charged on the loan, but the interest charged is credited back to the employee and the loan can be outstanding for as long as five years (or even longer if the loan was used to buy a home).

Q: *Are retirement plans a "good deal," particularly in light of eventually having to pay taxes along with the cumulative effects of inflation?*

The answer is an unequivocal "yes" for a number of reasons. First, study after study shows that the great majority of Americans lack the necessary discipline to save, particularly for retirement. Second, there is no indication that income tax rates will be higher when you retire than they are now; in fact, the overall trend over the past thirty-five years has been downward. Most retirement plans allow the participant to make large or small withdrawals annually, thereby allowing the retired employee to take out more money when he or she is in a lower bracket one year and less money in a high tax year.

Even though qualified retirement plans such as a 401(k) are one of the few remaining tax shelters, this does not mean that one's portfolio is sheltered from the cumulative effects of inflation. Nevertheless, the benefits of tax-deferred growth can be staggering. As an example, consider someone who is 25 years old and contributes $2,000 a year to an IRA for just five years. Assume that no additional contributions are made (a total of $10,000 is invested over a five-year period). Further assume that the contributions are invested in U.S. common stocks and that the future rate of growth is the same as it has averaged over the past fifty years (12 percent per year for the S&P 500). Finally, assume that the employee retires at age 65. You may be surprised to learn that the IRA will be worth $751,027.

True, thirty-five years from now (when the person in the example above will reach age 65), $751,027 will not have anywhere close to the purchasing power that it does today, but I would rather have the money than not have it. Furthermore, the actual investment was less than $10,000 when you include the $2,000 deduction the investor received for each of those five years. If the maximum 401(k) contribution (which was $9,240 in 1995) were made each year, the employee would end up with over $3,000,000 instead of $751,027.

Q: *Mentally, I have difficulty getting over the idea that my money is, for the most part, tied up until my employment is terminated or I reach age 59 1/2. Any suggestions to counter this concern?*

Yes. Keep in mind that the best investments require patience. People who have owned their own home for twenty or more years will attest to this. Rates of return fluctuate over the years, but there are a couple of certainties: (1) The cumulative effects of inflation are devastating, and (2) the older you get, the less flexibility or choice you have as to your future destiny and standard of living. In the final analysis, given time, a comfortable retirement is one of the few things you can plan on. It is obvious that employer- and government-sponsored benefits will continue to decrease in the future. You will need all the financial protection you can get. In other words, you really have no choice—ongoing contributions to a retirement plan are a requirement unless you are certain you are going to inherit a sizable estate.

Q: *Is my 401(k) account mine, or will it ever be commingled?*

No matter how large or small the company you work for, each participant (employee) has his or her own separate 401(k) account. Since these moneys and accounts are segregated, the financial solvency of the company you work for will have no bearing on the value or security of your account (unless you are invested in the company's stocks or bonds). Furthermore, the value or performance of your account will be similar to that of a coworker's account only if he or she happens to be investing in the same things you are. There is no commingling; the hiring or firing of employees will not affect your account's balance.

Q: *Are 401(k) plans insured?*

A 401(k) account is not insured per se, however, the investments you go into may be insured or backed by the government, by one of its agencies, or by an insurance company.

Q: *Are my 401(k) plan contributions subject to Social Security taxes?*

Yes. Contributions are usually free of federal, state, and local income taxes, but not Social Security taxes. Social Security taxes are levied on your gross pay, not just on the portion of your paycheck that remains after a deduction has been made for a 401(k).

Q: *Do I have to contribute to a 401(k) plan every quarter or every year?*

No. You may discontinue 401(k) contributions at any time, permanently or temporarily. Once you stop making contributions, any matching employer contributions will also cease (since there is nothing to match).

Q: *How long does my employer have between the time my paycheck is debited for my 401(k) contribution and the actual date when the money is invested on my behalf?*

By law, employers cannot delay such crediting for more than ninety days. If you ever have a complaint about the way your 401(k) plan is being handled and you are not getting satisfaction from the company you work for, contact the Department of Labor's Pension and Welfare Benefits Administration.

Q: *How does the IRS define "hardship" for purposes of making withdrawals prior to age 59 1/2?*

Hardships are defined as any one of the following: withdrawals necessary for (1) unreimbursed medical expenses, (2) college tuition bills for you, your spouse, or your children, (3) payment of threat of eviction or foreclosure if rent or mortgage payments are not made, and (4) purchase of a primary residence. If the money is used to purchase a home, you will probably be subject to a state and federal penalty, but at least the money can be taken out.

Besides what is allowed by the IRS, your company may expand upon this definition and include such hardship claims as (1) funeral expenses, (2) legal bills, and (3) loss of family income because of a *spouse's* being disabled or laid off from work.

Q: *If I want to make an early withdrawal, what do I do?*

First, contact your employer's employee benefits coordinator (this may be your company's financial officer). The person handling the 401(k) plan will tell you what forms need to be completed. Be prepared to wait up to two months.

Q: *Can I borrow money from my 401(k) instead of making an early withdrawal (which may or may not be subject to state and federal penalties)?*

Yes, if your company's 401(k) plan document includes provisions for loans. The beauty of loans, if they are allowed, is that there is no penalty and no tax and no need to prove or show hardship. Tax-free loans may be made for up to one-half of your 401(k) account balance or $50,000, *whichever is less*. Unless the loan is used to purchase a home, it must be paid back within five years. Repayment terms for the loan and the applicable interest rate being charged should be spelled out in the 401(k) documents (again, this assumes that your company's plan allows loans).

Q: *Assuming that I have an outstanding loan from my 401(k), do I get to deduct the interest on such a loan, even though the interest is being paid by me to me?*

No. Interest on personal loans is no longer tax-deductible. There is some comfort in knowing that any interest paid is credited to your account and that such interest and principal repayment will grow and compound tax-deferred.

Q: *Assuming that I cannot show "hardship" and I am under age 59 1/2, what kinds of penalties and taxes will I face if I make a premature withdrawal?*

In the absence of death, disability, or hardship, employees who make withdrawals before age 59 1/2 or termination of employment face a federal penalty of 10 percent plus any applicable state penalty (e.g., in California the penalty is 2.5 percent). As an example, assume that a California resident, age 45, has a 401(k) worth $35,000 and wants to take out

$10,000. The 401(k) participant cannot show hardship and has not had his or her employment terminated. First, there is the 10 percent federal penalty (10 percent of $10,000 = $1,000). Second, an additional $250 will be subtracted to satisfy the state of California (2.5 percent of $10,000). Third, the resident will be required to pay state and federal income taxes for the calendar year in which the withdrawal is made (meaning that $10,000 will be added to his or her other sources of taxable income). The added income will be $10,000 in this example, not $10,000 minus any penalties incurred.

Q: *How does the IRS define "disabled" for purposes of being able to take money out of a qualified retirement plan before age 59 1/2 without penalty?*

To qualify as being disabled, you must be both incapacitated and unable to work. A doctor's certification is usually enough proof. If you are disabled and wish to take money out of your Keogh, 401(k), IRA, or other qualified retirement plan, make sure you inform the institution overseeing your account of your disability. With such notification and certification, the trustee of your retirement plan, when issuing you a 1099R for the year, will fill in Box 7 with a Code 3. This way, the IRS is alerted to the situation and will not penalize you. If the institution does not do this, you should file IRS Form 5329 to claim the disability exemption. Income taxes are still due on these withdrawals, but at least there will not be a state or federal penalty.

Q: *When am I required to take money out of my 401(k)?*

In order to avoid a 50 percent penalty, your first withdrawal must be no later than April 1 of the year following the year you reached age 70 1/2. This means that if you became age 70 1/2 on January 1, 1996, you could postpone the withdrawal until April 1, 1997.

Q: *Once I retire, how much do I have to take out of my 401(k) each year?*

Until you reach age 70 1/2, no withdrawals are required. From age 59 1/2 to 70 1/2 you have complete flexibility: You can make withdrawals of any amount; there is no minimum and no maximum. Once you reach age 70 1/2, at least minimum withdrawals must be made. The amount that must be withdrawn at least once a year is based on IRS life expectancy tables. The number of years can be extended if your spouse or someone younger than you are is named as the beneficiary. As an example, a 70-year-old man has a remaining life expectancy of close to fifteen years, meaning that about one-fifteenth of his retirement accounts must be liquidated each year. If this same man had a wife who was age 65, the IRS would require that only about one-twentieth be taken out each year (since a combined lives table would be used).

Q: *One of my children has applied for college financial aid. If I withdraw money from my 401(k), will it affect the child's chances of receiving student aid?*

Yes. For tax purposes, the IRS treats withdrawals as ordinary income, and such withdrawals are included as part of your taxable income for the year. Instead of a withdrawal, consider a loan, which is not included as taxable income and will not affect your child's chances of getting financial aid.

Q: *Can I move my 401(k) account from one employer to another?*

Yes. In order to avoid a 20 percent withholding tax, make sure that you do not have constructive receipt of the moneys. In other words, make sure that the transfer is direct and that no check is made out to you; instead, the check should be made out to the trustee of the new qualified retirement plan that you are about to enter.

Q: *Am I required to transfer my existing 401(k) to an IRA or my next employer?*

No. Unless the account is valued at $3,500 or less, you may leave it with your previous employer until you reach the age of retirement, as defined in the company's plan documents.

Q: *I have recently changed jobs. My new employer will not let me participate in the company's 401(k) plan for several months, and my old company will not let me let me leave the money where it is now. What can I do?*

Have your former employer transfer your 401(k) account into an IRA of your choosing. Later, once you meet the new company's 401(k) requirements, you can have the IRA account transferred. Make sure that you do not add to this temporary IRA account.

Q: *How many retirement plans can I have in addition to a 401(k)?*

It depends. At the very least, you can also set up an IRA (the contribution may or may not be tax-deductible depending upon your adjusted gross income). You may also take advantage of any other retirement plans offered to you by your employer. Additionally, if you have a business of your own, you may also be able to set up and contribute to a Keogh.

Q: *If I do not contribute to my company's 401(k), but my employer does contribute on my behalf, can I still have an IRA and deduct my IRA contributions?*

Perhaps. If your employer is making contributions on your behalf, you may not be able to deduct your IRA contributions—deductibility will depend upon your adjusted gross income (AGI), or the combined AGI of both you and your spouse if you are married.

Q: *Given the choice, is it better to roll over my 401(k) into my new employer's 401(k) or into an IRA?*

Most retirement accounts, such as a 401(k), may be eligible for five- or ten-year income averaging upon retirement. Normally, an IRA does not qualify for such income averaging. However, money rolled over from a 401(k) into an IRA can qualify for income averaging as long as this IRA account is not "tainted" with other IRA contributions or accounts.

From an investment perspective, your decision to move money into an IRA or into a new 401(k) should be based upon the number of investment choices offered by each plan, the amount of time you or your financial adviser is willing to devote to the IRA, and the caliber of money management offered by the new 401(k) plan.

Q: *I am about to retire and plan on transferring my 401(k) account into an IRA. I am not sure what to do, since part of the 401(k) represents after-tax dollar contributions (meaning that there was no deduction for these dollars).*

By law you are *required* to segregate and remove all after-tax dollar contributions (but not the growth or interest represented by such contributions); only the balance may be transferred into an IRA. The good news is that these after-tax contributions will not be taxed to you when you take them out, and there is no penalty. It is your employer's responsibility to keep track of your contributions and to be able to distinguish between pre- and after-tax dollar contributions made on your behalf.

Q: *My 401(k) includes both pre- and after-tax contributions. I am about to retire and want to roll the account into an IRA, but my boss is either unable or unwilling to separate the contributions. What should I do?*

Rollover the entire 401(k) into an IRA. You should then

withdraw the after-tax portion (without penalty or tax) by justifying such withdrawals as a "correction of excess contribution." You should contact the IRS and tell them of the problem (since you probably do not know what the exact figure is) and consider contacting the Department of Labor.

Q: *I left my job several months ago and I still have not received money from my 401(k) plan. How long can my former employer delay such a distribution?*

Surprisingly, there is no legal deadline; however, the distribution schedule should be detailed in the company's 401(k) plan documents. Delays of over a year are not uncommon, since your request for distribution may have been made just after the 401(k) plan year ended (which is often different from the end of a calendar year). Appeal procedures for such delays should be outlined in the company's summary plan description, another document that you are entitled to receive. Finally, if all else fails, you may contact the Department of Labor.

Q: *What is the difference between a 401(k) and a 403(b) plan?*

Public schools and charitable organizations, including nonprofit hospitals, offer 403(b) plans because they are not allowed to offer 401(k) plans. A 403(b) may invest only in annuities. A 401(k) may allow investments in annuities, life insurance, bank CDs, government securities, individual stocks and bonds, and a wide array of mutual funds.

Q: *Who do I contact if I want more information about a 401(k) or investments in general?*

Listed below are some sources you may wish to contact if you have any questions about your 401(k) plan:

1. Your employer
2. The person listed as broker of record on your account statement

3. Mutual fund or insurance companies whose products are included as options within your plan

4. The 401(k) Association (call 215-579-8830 or write to: One Summit Square, Doublewoods Road, Route 413, Langhorne, PA 19047)

5. The Institute of Certified Fund Specialists (call 800-848-2029 or write to: ICFS, 7911 Herschel Avenue, Suite 201, La Jolla, CA 92037).

Index

ALSO BY GORDON WILLIAMSON

Low Risk Investing
How to get a good return on your money
without losing any sleep.
Trade paperback, 352 pp., $9.95

In *Low Risk Investing*, Williamson clearly and concise-
ly explains the many sound alternatives for achieving a
good return on your money with minimal risk. He rates
each investment vehicle for security of principal, stability
of income, total return, tax consequences, and as a hedge
against inflation. Williamson also defines each investment,
outlines its advantages and disadvantages, and details
how the instrument is bought and sold.

The 100 Best Mutual Funds You Can Buy
Trade paperback, 304 pp., $12.95

Updated yearly! Williamson systematically re-evalu-
ates every one of the over 3,000 mutual funds on the
market to determine an authoritative ranking of the top
100. Each fund is analyzed for total return, risk, quality
of management, current income, and expense control.
Includes money market funds.

Available Wherever Books Are Sold

ABOUT THE AUTHOR

Gordon K. Williamson, JD, MB, MS, CFP, CLU, ChFC, RP, is one of the most highly trained investment counselors in the United States. Williamson, a former tax attorney, is a Certified Financial Planner and branch manager of a national brokerage firm. He has been admitted to The Registry of Financial Planning Practitioners, the highest honor one can attain as a financial planner. He holds the two highest designations in the life insurance industry, Chartered Life Underwriter and Chartered Financial Consultant. He is also a real estate broker with an MBA in real estate.

Mr. Williamson is the founder and executive director of the Institute of Certified Fund Specialists, a professional education program that leads to the designation "CFS" (800-848-2029).

He is also the author of twenty books, including *The 100 Best Annuities You Can Buy*, *The 401(k) Book*, *All about Annuities*, *How You Can Survive under Clinton/Gore*, *The Longman Investment Companion*, *Investment Strategies*, *Survey of Financial Planning*, *Tax Shelters*, *Advanced Investment Vehicles and Techniques*, *Your Living Trust*, *The 100 Best Mutual Funds You Can Buy*, *Sooner than You Think*, and *Low-Risk Investing*. He has been the financial editor of various magazines and newspapers and a stock market consultant for a television station.

Gordon K. Williamson is an investment advisory firm located in La Jolla, California. The firm specializes in financial planning for individuals and institutions ($100,000 minimum account size). Additional information can be obtained by phoning 800-748-5552 or 619-454-3938.